# Moral Manhood

## Swimming with the Sharks

### DR. BOB ABRAMSON

MENTORING MINISTRY
Dr. Bob Abramson

Moral Manhood - Swimming with the Sharks
Published by Alphabet Resources, Inc.
365 Stonehenge Drive
Phillipsburg, NJ 08865
1-561-963-0778
Dr.Bob@mentoringministry.com

Unless otherwise specified, the following applies to all Scripture quotes. Scripture taken from the New King James Version. Copyright © 1982 by Thomas Nelson, Inc. Used by permission. All rights reserved.

Scripture quotations marked (NLT) are taken from the Holy Bible, New Living Translation, copyright © 1996, 2004, 2007. Used by permission of Tyndale House Publishers, Inc., Carol Stream, Illinois 60188. All rights reserved.

Scripture quotations marked (NIV) are taken from the Holy Bible, New International Version®, NIV®. Copyright © 1973, 1978, 1984 by Biblica, Inc.™ Used by permission of Zondervan. All rights reserved worldwide. www.zondervan.com

GOD'S WORD is a copyrighted work of God's Word to the Nations. Quotations are used by permission. Copyright 1995 by God's Word to the Nations. All rights reserved.

Cover design by Ryan Stacey

10 digit ISBN 0-9843443-7-3
13 digit ISBN 978-0-9843443-7-6
Library of Congress Control Number: 2011915144

Contact Dr. Abramson by visiting
www.mentoringministry.com

# CONTENTS

Introduction

# Understanding Your Manhood
## (Real Man, Husband, Father, Leader... or Wimp?)

# Your World: Uniquely Yours

In many ways, every man's world is the same. It is filled with commitments, challenging relationships and undeniable pressures. None of us escapes. We all face them. However, your world is not identical to mine. It is uniquely yours. We each have our own distinct limits and boundaries. These restrain our abilities, gifts, and motivations. We may, or may not be aware of them, but limitations are part of life. They come in two packages. First, some outside force may impose them upon us. Second, they may be imposed on us from within.

What you will be reading is designed to help you identify, confront and break through limitations that may have kept you from greater measures of success and restrained you from the fullness of your own manhood. As you read through the book, you will be challenged with a specific goal: to go past your limitations to be all you are called to be - a moral man and a champion before the Lord.

You can go a long way toward taking the limits off your life if you will take a wrecking ball to some of your thinking. God is interested in renovating the way you think and reconstructing it according to His thinking. This may not be easy or comfortable. Usually, men of God are called to think like builders, not wreckers, but some of our thinking needs wrecking, rebuilding or renovating. Renovators are men of courage, not wimps. The Apostle Paul understood this, as he wrote the following to the Roman church.

> *(Romans 12:1-3 NKJV) "I beseech you therefore, brethren, by the mercies of God, that you present your bodies a living sacrifice, holy, acceptable to God, which is your reasonable service. {2} And do not be conformed to this world, but be transformed by the renewing of your mind, that you may prove what is that good and acceptable and perfect will of God. {3} For I say, through the grace given to me, to everyone who is among you, not to think of himself more highly than he ought to think, but to think soberly, as God has dealt to each one a measure of faith."*

# A Better Understanding of Manhood

## (What should be a distinguishing feature of your manhood?)

Jesus established undemanding love as the primary and universal characteristic of a Christian man. He described and modeled this love as pure and purely given, with no motivation for selfish return. The Lord commanded that unselfish love be seen and demonstrated in us. The distinguishing feature of your manhood should be undemanding love.

> *(Matthew 22:37-39 NKJV) "Jesus said to him, 'You shall love the LORD your God with all your heart, with all your soul, and with all your mind.' {38} This is the first and great commandment. {39} And the second is like it: 'You shall love your neighbor as yourself.'"*

> *(Luke 6:35 NKJV) "But love your enemies, do good, and lend, hoping for nothing in return; and your reward will be great, and you will be sons of the Most High."*

---

### LIFELINE

The character of manhood is defined by undemanding love.

---

Manhood ought to be a life of service and ministry characterized by undemanding love. Dr. Lawrence O. Richards, in his "Expository Dictionary of Biblical Words," gives insight into the New Testament Greek words for *"ministering"* and *"ministry."* He says the following.

> "These words are distinctive in that their focus is squarely on loving action... there is a sense in which every believer is a minister and is to use his or her gifts to serve others. Loving action characterized by the use of our gifts to serve others is what we do, because it imitates the example of Christ, pleases God, and makes a difference in our world."[1]

> *(Matthew 25:34-40 NKJV) "Then the King will say to those on His right hand, Come, you blessed of My Father, inherit the kingdom prepared for you from the foundation of the world: {35} for I was hungry and you gave Me food; I was thirsty and you gave Me drink; I was a stranger and you took Me in; {36} I was naked and you clothed Me; I was sick and you visited Me: I was in prison and you came to Me.' {37} Then the righteous will answer Him, saying, 'Lord, when did we see You hungry and feed you or thirsty and give You drink? {38} When did we see You a stranger and take You*

---

[1] Richards, Lawrence O., <u>Expository Dictionary of Bible Words</u>, The Zondervan Corporation, Grand Rapids, 1985, PP.443-444.

*in, or naked and clothe You? {39} Or when did we see You sick, or in prison, and come to You?' {40} And the King will answer and say to them, 'Assuredly, I say to you, inasmuch as you did it to one of the least of these My brethren, you did it to Me.'"*

Your manhood ought to be a reflection of your commitment to please, honor and bless the Lord. You show this by your service to Him through what you do for others, with undemanding love.

## Pride - A Manhood Eating Monster

(What should <u>not</u> be a distinguishing feature of your manhood?)

One thing that should <u>not</u> be a distinguishing feature of your manhood is pride. Will you be a real man of God, or a prideful wimp? Let's look at four biblical examples of men whose pride disqualified them from moral manhood. The results were devastating and tragic. These four were Shechem, King Saul, King Solomon and Samson.

## Four Familiar Wimps with One Common Problem

*I have these wimps acting just like me!*

5

# Wimp #1 - Shechem

*(Genesis 34:1-3 NKJV) "Now Dinah the daughter of Leah, whom she had borne to Jacob, went out to see the daughters of the land. {2} And when Shechem the son of Hamor the Hivite, prince of the country, saw her, he took her and lay with her, and violated her. {3} His soul was strongly attracted to Dinah the daughter of Jacob, and he loved the young woman and spoke kindly to the young woman."*

What disqualified Shechem and made him a pride-filled wimp and not a real man? The answer is not difficult to see. Shechem's pride caused him to misuse his manhood to manipulate Dinah by dominating and abusing her for his personal, sexual satisfaction. He was a worthless lustbag who paid for his attitude with his life. In the process, he ruined Dinah's reputation and destroyed the lives of others.

A challenge for every man is how we look at and treat the women in our lives. Whether you are married, single, or single again, you have an opportunity to be a morally strong, righteous man in your attitudes and actions toward women. Let your life honor God and reflect the principles of His Word.

# Wimp #2 - King Saul

*(1 Samuel 18:6-11 NKJV) "Now it had happened as they were coming home, when David was returning from the slaughter of the Philistine, that the women had come out of all the cities of Israel, singing and dancing, to meet King Saul, with tambourines, with joy, and with musical instruments. {7} So the women sang as they danced, and said: "Saul has slain his thousands, And David his ten thousands." {8} Then Saul was very angry, and the saying displeased him; and he said, "They have ascribed to David ten thousands, and to me they have ascribed only thousands. Now what more can he have but the kingdom?" {9} So Saul eyed David from that day forward. {10} And it happened on the next day that the distressing spirit from God came upon Saul, and he prophesied inside the house. So David played music with his hand, as at other times; but there was a spear in Saul's hand. {11} And Saul cast the spear, for he said, "I will pin David to the wall!" But David escaped his presence twice."*

What made King Saul a prideful wimp and not a real man? Saul's pride invited strongholds of demonic jealousy, anger and depression into his life. These strongholds caused him to exercise evil judgment with the authority he possessed. He was not content to find his significance and satisfaction in the place God had appointed him. He failed to trust God and feared that David might take away what he had come to covet. It cost him everything.

## Wimp #3 - King Solomon

*(1 Kings 11:1-4, 9 and 11 NKJV) "But King Solomon loved many foreign women... {2} from the nations of whom the LORD had said to the children of Israel, "You shall not intermarry with them, nor they with you. Surely they will turn away your hearts after their gods." Solomon clung to these in love. {3} And he had seven hundred wives, princesses, and three hundred concubines; and his wives turned away his heart. {4} ...and his heart was not loyal to the LORD his God, as was the heart of his father David... {9} So the LORD became angry with Solomon, because his heart had turned from the LORD God of Israel... {11} Therefore the LORD said to Solomon, "Because you have done this, and have not kept My covenant and My statutes, which I have commanded you, I will surely tear the kingdom away from you and give it to your servant."*

What got King Solomon into trouble and made him a prideful wimp and not a real man? His disqualifying mistakes were twofold. First, he was disobedient to the Lord. He had a disloyal heart. Second, he dishonored the gift of wisdom God had granted to him. In his pride, he forgot that it was God who had given him the power to get his wealth. The wisest man in the world did the dumbest things imaginable because he stopped fearing God. What a wimp!

## Wimp #4 - Samson

Samson

*(Judges 16:4-6 and 16-17 NKJV) "Afterward it happened that he loved a woman in the Valley of Sorek, whose name was Delilah. {5} And the lords of the Philistines came up to her and said to her, "Entice him, and find out where his great strength lies, and by what means we may overpower him, that we may bind him to afflict him; and every one of us will give you eleven hundred pieces of silver." {6} So Delilah said to Samson, "Please tell me where your great strength lies, and with what you may be bound to afflict you... {16} And it came to pass, when she pestered him daily with her words and pressed him, so that his soul was vexed to death, {17} that he told her all his heart... "If I am shaven, then my strength will leave me, and I shall become weak, and be like any other man.""*

What made Samson a wimp and not a real man? He was so sure of himself that he foolishly revealed the secret of his strength to Delilah. It was his downfall. His pride got the best of him. It deceived him to the point that he thought his great physical strength and ability to dominate others would keep him safe and successful. He was disqualified because he failed to remember his commitment to and dependence on God. The rest is history. He forgot the Lord his God. He was a real wimp and a pitiful loser!

Shechem, Saul, Solomon and Sampson all chose pride over humility and obedience to God. It was their downfall. They were disqualified. Pride will do that to any man who replaces humility before the Lord with his own pride.

## Samswim: A Winner and a Champion
### (A Real Man)

Where is the power to be a real man, husband, father and leader? In the pages that follow, you will discover the answer as you meet a little guy whose name is Samswim (yes, Samswim, not Samson). Samswim is our example of a real man of God, who is a winner and a champion for Jesus.

Samswim

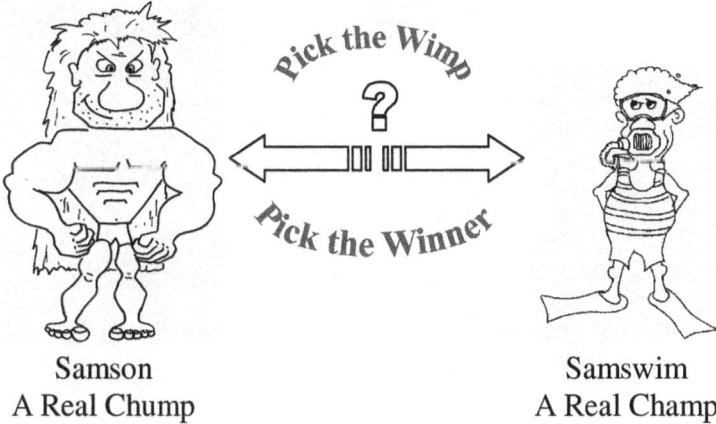

Samson
A Real Chump

Samswim
A Real Champ

In Chapter 1, we will look more closely at pride. All four of our wimps found out the hard way that pride is a man-eating monster that prowls the depths of a man's mind and emotions. Pride, like a shark on the hunt, has no pity, gives no mercy and loves a sneak attack. Often, we find ourselves in the grip of its jaws and suffer the consequences before we realize it was there. Like a hungry shark, it seeks to sink its teeth into any available target it can find.

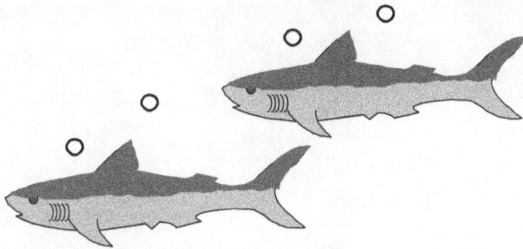

You are about to take a swim through shark-infested waters, but fear not. Samswim will lead the way. He will point us to God, who supplies all that we need to keep ourselves safe from this monster called pride, and from many of the other issues we face as men. We will explore ways you can change your perspective about yourself, others and God so that you can face all the sharks of life. Men, grab your goggles and let's go swimming!

# Part I

# SWIMMING WITH THE SHARKS

# Chapter 1

## Shark Cages

### (Places to Hide from Pride)

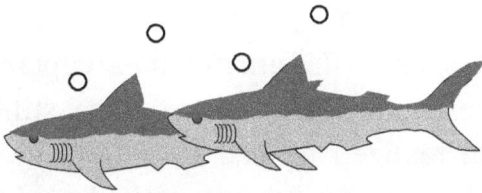

## The Dangers of Swimming with Sharks

What follows is a true story that happened just before my wife Nancy and I came back to America from our missionary work in Fiji in 1998.

A husband and wife, who were Peace Corps workers in Fiji, had just completed their tour of duty. They decided to take an around-the-world trip on their way back to America. Their first stop was Australia, where they were going to do some diving on the Great Barrier Reef. They, along with a number of others, took a charter boat tour out to the Reef. When they arrived, everyone went diving for the day.

The charter boat stayed at anchor, and the captain assured them that he would be waiting for them when the day came to a close. The group would then be returned safely to port. True to his word, the captain remained on station throughout the day. At the appropriate time, he helped everyone get back into the boat... well, almost everyone. He neglected to count the returning divers and verify they all were there.

Two days later, the charter boat captain found the American couple's belongings still on the boat. He realized he had forgotten the couple. They had not come back with the rest of his passengers. He had left them out in the middle of the ocean on the Great Barrier Reef! This part of the ocean is home to the great white shark, the most ferocious and dangerous animal in the world.

The charter boat captain returned to the spot on the reef where he had left them. He searched, but to no avail. All that was eventually found were a few bits and pieces of their diving gear that washed up on shore, along with their diving slate. We heard that it had this message scrawled on it: *"Can you help us? We have been abandoned. Please rescue us before we die!"* Sadly, they were never seen again.

Can you imagine what it must have felt like when they surfaced and saw there was no boat? They had no refuge, no place to go and nowhere to hide. They had to swim with the sharks. Imagine the terror they felt. They would have given anything for a shark cage… anything!

## A Life of Moral Manhood

A life of moral manhood can be compared to swimming in the waters off the Great Barrier Reef. These waters are deep and full of hungry sharks. Life for every man is, in many ways, just like that. The environment of today's society is so full of risks to his integrity and wholeness, that it is necessary to have the protection of a divine shark cage at all times. Otherwise, he is moral shark bait!

Every man needs God's divine provision of His heavenly shark cages to avoid being eaten by the hungry predators of daily life. Chief among these is the lurking monster of pride.

*(Proverbs 16:18 NKJV) "Pride goes before destruction, And a haughty spirit before a fall."*

*(Proverbs 16:25 NKJV) "There is a way that seems right to a man, But its end is the way of death."*

The toughest man in the world cannot swim with sharks without being bitten. Only a prideful and ignorant man would jump in the middle of a bunch of hungry sharks, thinking he is immune. Have you ever met the shark called pride? Of course you have. You may be swimming with him as you read this.

What did you see in the mirror this morning, as you prepared for the day? Was it someone who walked a little bit in Samson's shoes (or sandals)?

- How often have you seen the disappointment or hurt in the eyes of someone who was eaten up by your need to have your own prideful way?

  Mr. Selfishness, always says, *"I want mine first,"* which actually means, *"I do not really care about anyone else."*

- Has pride caused you not to listen to someone God sent to stop you from wimping out to the devil?

  Mr. Defiled is seldom particular about what he allows to have a home inside of him. He opens his mind and heart to so much shark bait, that he is easy prey. He is attracted to everything the world throws at him and never realizes he is becoming the bait, until he feels the gripping pain of pride's harsh bite.

- Has your pride gotten you into an avoidable confrontation because it had control of your mouth? Have bitter words ever come out of you because someone criticized you, disagreed with you or challenged you?
- Do you value being right more than anything?
- Is maintaining your pride more important than what it does to your relationships?
- How many times have prideful mistakes caused you to miss opportunities?
- Are you as teachable as you could be? If not, you are surely missing the opportunity to gain wisdom and understanding. One of the primary characteristics of pride is its ability to restrict or deny the truth.

God supplies all we need to keep ourselves safe from this monster called pride. God's "shark cages" are custom-built place to hide from pride. They are uniquely and divinely designed for the particular waters in which we swim. They provide us with safety zones in which to be better men, husbands, fathers and leaders. They keep us within God's will for our lives, and set boundaries for our attitudes, actions and experiences. They are structures or places of humility where God's protection surrounds us. When properly respected, they are always strong enough to keep away the predator called pride.

# Raw Materials for Shark Cages

Let's talk about these places of safety from pride, the divine shark cages that God makes available to you. They are strong enough to keep you safe, because they are constructed of sure, tough, dependable components. Let's look at some of these.

## 1. Your Conscience

Every man has an inner sense of right and wrong. This inhibits us from doing what is morally

✝ "It is well." ✝

improper and offensive to God. However, if we allow pride to deaden our consciences, the strength of our shark cages deteriorates. There will be nowhere to hide from pride. A moral man values the inner voice of his conscience, knowing it will keep him humble and clear-headed, well able to navigate the issues of life.

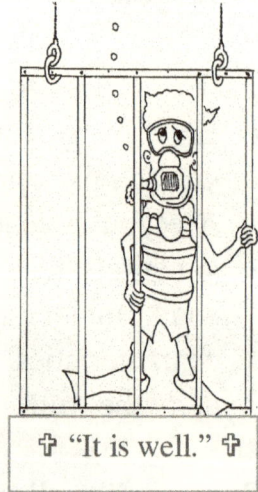

## 2. Relationships with Godly Men

This is a vital component to a moral man's safety. Pride tries to convince us to ignore what others have to say and go with our own thoughts and feelings. Doing so eliminates the opportunity to hear sound,

wise advice from those who care enough to speak it.
Strengthen your relationships with other men of God.
Add this to your commitment to God and you have an
accountability structure that becomes far stronger than
the every-day temptations and circumstances that try
to get to you. Be sure you nurture and submit to your
relationships. They will provide the insulation you
need from life's shark bites.

## 3. Knowledge of Your Weaknesses

It is often easy to see another man's weaknesses, but
be blinded to our own. One of the most profitable
things you can do for yourself is to be aware of what
might tempt or test you because it preys on a
particular weakness. Denial is dangerous. Knowing
your weaknesses greatly strengthens your shark cage.

## 4. Your Relationship with God

Your commitment to your relationship with God must
begin with your heart. It must be absolutely without
compromise. Determine to commit yourself to be a
man after God's own heart, as David was (1 Samuel
13:14). Surround yourself with this commitment.
Lock yourself into it. Deepen your relationship with
the Holy Spirit. He will be your ever-present help.

## 5. A Healthy Fear of the Lord

This is perhaps the most important component.
Keeping yourself aware of the holy, sovereign God

you serve will keep the gate to the shark cage shut when pride attacks. Make the fear of the Lord indispensable. It is the beginning of wisdom. It will provide you with a divine Lifeguard, who has more than enough weapons to drive every shark away. The fear of the Lord is the true strength of moral manhood. We will explore this again in Chapters 4 and 5.

## 6. Your Relationship with the Word of God

Your relationship with the Word of God forms the welds that hold your shark cage together. Therefore, the quality of this relationship determines the strength or weakness of your shark cage. This relationship has the potential to tie the other five elements into an impenetrable fortress that the sharks of life cannot get through. It does this by providing the moral man with access to God's wisdom. Your relationship with the Word is your best, and ought to be your primary source of this wisdom. Use it wisely and it will insure your ability to make sound decisions, which will guide you concerning the waters of life in which you must swim. Hebrews 4:12 assures us the Word of God is a *"powerful"* weapon. It will stun the sharks in your life and leave them without the teeth to inflict trouble on you.

## Additional Components of Your Shark Cage

We will continue to add components of your shark cage, but for now, examine your heart. You will likely find other components available to you that will further strengthen your shark cage. Take advantage of them. Let them be your constant companions.

## Every Man a Swimmer
### (Will you be like Samson or Samswim?)

We all have the challenge of living in a world that requires us to swim in evil waters. This does not mean you have to swallow any, or invite what is swimming in it to be attracted to you. You will find the world and much of what is in it to be a test of your manhood. Will you stand in your shark cage filled with appreciation for God's grace? If the bars of your particular cage do not include the fear of the Lord, you are swimming into some very big jaws. Do not be a chump. Be a champ! Look at the words of Jonathan Edwards.

*"There us nothing that keeps wicked men at any one moment out of hell, but the mere pleasure of God... I mean his sovereign pleasure, his arbitrary will, restrained by no obligation ..."*[3]

## Do not wimp out!

---

[3]Jonathan Edwards on Knowing Christ, a reprint of Select Works of Jonathan Edwards Vol.2, 1958, (from the 1839 London edition of Edwards' Works), The Banner of Truth Trust, Edinburgh, 1990, P.184.

# Stay in the Cage.

All men must navigate the sinful streams of life. God has given you the shark cage to keep you from being devoured by that vicious and unrelenting predator called pride. God's grace will make a way for you to discover His "places to hide from pride." These are part of His provision to make a man out of you and keep you from wimping out!

Where is that cage?

Wimp Sharkbait!

Samson
(Sam-*sin*)

Every moral man's constant challenge and ever-present frustration is trying to live a spiritual life in an evil, carnal world. You will face daily, even hourly challenges from the evils that surround you. You will also face challenges from within you. There are those times when you will swim in your own successes. Success is a powerful invitation to pride. However, you can survive the pride that accompanies success. Just keep humility as your way of escape.

Whether the challenges are from without or within, they can be a powerful source of tension for a man who is doing his best to serve the Lord. We all have taken swims in our own successes and failures. With God, we do not have to drown in them or become fish food for the pride sharks. It is always your choice to reject the sin and draw closer to God. When you stay fixed on Christ, the shark cannot bite. Just keep loving and serving God.

> *(Romans 8:28 NKJV) "And we know that all things work together for good to those who love God, to those who are the called according to His purpose."*

All things, including your own successes and failures, can work together for good if you fit the description of a Romans 8:28 man. Do you love God? Is Christ the absolute authority over everything you face? He is the divine dispenser of both grace and judgment. As a moral man, you can swim securely among the currents of life, knowing that with God, the evils you face daily will not ultimately prevail. You are in His care. Even when you think you might be failing, or when you have a lapse in your own commitment, just swim back to God. He will open the door to His divine shark cage. Whether the attack is from the shark outside the cage, or something fishy from within, you have God's assurance everything will be OK.

Here is my advice. Stay in the cage. Do not compromise concerning with whom or what you swim. The god of this world is reaching for you with jaws open wide. Do not encourage him and make his efforts easier. We probably all do this to some degree. Think about it. Satan and his lies are only stopped when we, as men of God, refuse to wimp out! Get into your shark cage. Stand there in the truth of God's Word. Within this place of safety in an ocean filled with danger, you will find strength to resist the devil and the boldness to stand for Christ.

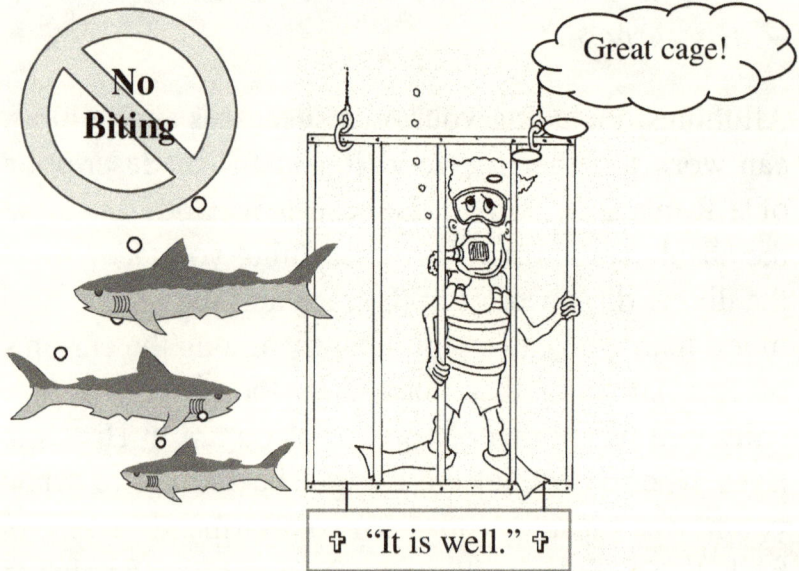

## Chapter 2

# The Morality Slide

Morality today is on the move,
                              sliding
                         ⇘⇘⇘   downward!
                         ⇘⇘⇘⇘⇘

Consider the world around you. It is apparent that in our societies and among so many of the men in them, the standards of morality are constantly moving downward.

Your effectiveness as a man of character and honor depends on your ability to identify, clearly and correctly, God's timeless truths. However, the water gets cloudier daily. The sharks have stirred it up. A man's values seem more and more difficult to define. The question becomes, can you stay focused on the integrity of God's truth without slipping into the morality slide? It is not always easy. The danger is that you might miss the truth and become party to Satan's lies.

Do not allow yourself to swim with the sharks. Doing so will cause you to become a predator, just like them.

Prideful, predatory relationships destroy families, friends, churches, societies... *and* the predators. A man who misuses his authority as father, husband or leader can become the biggest fish on his reef, with the biggest bite. As you descend the slippery slope of the morality slide, your bite will consume others... but beware, you are still shark bait, even as you bite others!

*That little fish won't bite me. I'm too tough!*

*This fool will make a good snack!*

Samson, also known as "Sharkbait Sam"

## Only a fool swims with sharks.

There are always bigger sharks than you swimming out there. If you let your morality slide, you will become no better than shark bait, pinned to the hook, limited and tied to a line. How does this happen?

1. You enter into spiritual poverty by rejecting God's truths. In doing so, you limit yourself to the ways of the world.

2. You accept the present limitations on your life and believe they cannot be changed. The world will tell you that you cannot make it; you cannot do it; you

are not able. Have you ever felt that way? Feeling sorry for yourself is simply the pride of self-pity.

3. You embrace the temptation to sin. You bite the apple. Then, the shark bites you. Now you become like what bit you, adept at biting into the lives of others.

4. You accept your prideful ways as inevitable and comfortable. You become so comfortable in your sins that you decide the effort to change is not worth it. Your opinion of yourself and your chances to fulfill the will of God sink into an ocean of inevitability.

5. Finally, you arrive at the place where you have given your state of spiritual poverty a lasting home. You live within it and allow it to dictate your life. You have hit the bottom of the slide.

Samson hit bottom and became shark bait when he exchanged his reverence for God for prideful worship of self.

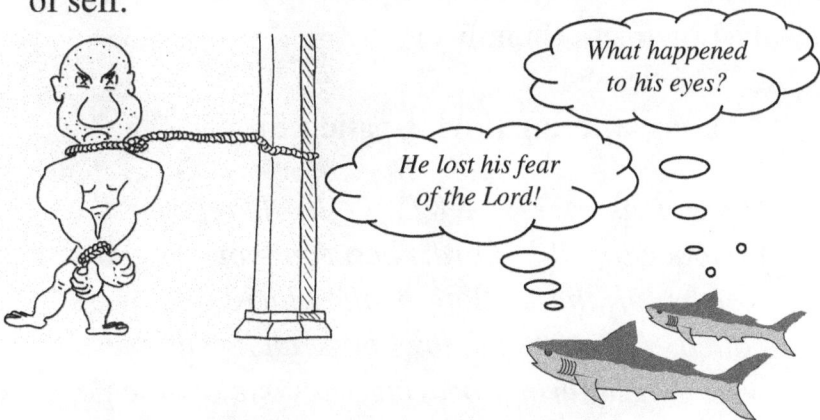

*Judges 16:20b (NKJV) "But he did not know that the LORD had departed from him."*

29

The proper response to a morality slide begins and ends with the fear of the Lord. Jesus is your answer. He is the Alpha and Omega and everything in-between. He is the A to Z, and the LMNOP! You will avoid spiritual blindness and safely swim past the sharks of life by maintaining a lifestyle of reverence for God and obedience to His Word.

*(Proverbs 1:7 NKJV) "The fear of the LORD is the beginning of knowledge, But fools despise wisdom and instruction."*

## Characteristics of a Moral Man

God provides clear instructions on how to be a man who is committed to personal morality. These instructions begin with Ephesians 4:1-3. They will help to keep you from slipping down the morality slide.

1. Lowliness (humility)
2. Gentleness
3. Longsuffering (loving patience)

*(Ephesians 4:1-3 NKJV) "I, therefore, the prisoner of the Lord, beseech you to walk worthy of the calling with which you were called, {2} with all lowliness and gentleness, with longsuffering, bearing with one another in love, {3} endeavoring to keep the unity of the Spirit in the bond of peace."*

By your humble, gentle, loving and patient actions (secured with the bond of peace), you will become an outward demonstration of the Christ-like character of a moral man.

## Instructions for a Moral Man

*(Ephesians 4:25-32 NKJV) "Therefore, putting away lying, Let each one of you speak truth with his neighbor, for we are members of one another. {26} Be angry, and do not sin: do not let the sun go down on your wrath, {27} nor give place to the devil. {28} Let him who stole steal no longer, but rather let him labor, working with his hands what is good, that he may have something to give him who has need. {29} Let no corrupt word proceed out of your mouth, but what is good for necessary edification, that it may impart grace to the hearers. {30} And do not grieve the Holy Spirit of God, by whom you were sealed for the day of redemption. {31} Let all bitterness, wrath, anger, clamor, and evil speaking be put away from you, with all malice. {32} And be kind to one another, tenderhearted, forgiving one another, just as God in Christ forgave you."*

1. Speak the Truth… always!
2. Deny the devil any room in your heart.
3. Make it your habit to thank God for everything that is yours and covet nothing from anyone else.
4. When you speak, be sure to speak words of encouragement and edification. Lift someone's spirits by speaking positive, enriching words, that bring forth God's grace and truth.
5. Release your anger.
6. Be kind toward those around you.
7. Soften your heart toward others. Be a man of forgiveness. Do not allow self-justification to capture you in unforgiveness toward others. You will only hurt yourself. (Also, be sure to forgive yourself. Too many of us spend far too much time living in our past mistakes. When you gave your life to Christ, your mistakes were pinned to the cross. They are no longer pinned to you.)

If you desire to swim safely through the currents of life, become a Colossians 3 Christian.

> *(Colossians 3:1-2 NKJV) "If then you were raised with Christ, seek those things which are above, where Christ is, sitting at the right hand of God. {2} Set your mind on things above, not on things on the earth…"*

Seek God and fill your mind with His Word. *"Set your mind on things above."* Too often, we set our thinking on the sharks, not understanding that there is a greater power within us that is sourced from above. We certainly need to be aware of our circumstances and the context of what we swim in, but it is a question of focus. When we look to Christ and all of His protection and provision, our focus gives us entrance into that divine shark cage. This is right thinking. It will keep us from sliding into the ways and consequences of wrong thinking.

## A Moral Man's Swimming Attire

*(Colossians 3:12b NLT) "...you must clothe yourselves with tenderhearted mercy, kindness, humility, gentleness, and patience."*

The list of swimming attire is specific. Clothe yourself in the following, in preparation for your daily swim with the sharks that are within and around you.

### Tender Mercies

It would be wrong to pass by this first article of swimming attire without understanding that the Holy Spirit inspired Paul to write of mercy as *"tenderhearted."* The message every Samswim needs to understand is that when mercy flows from anything but a tender, compassionate heart, it is not acceptable. Being merciful out of a sense of obligation or self-righteousness is simply an imitation of the world's way of being merciful. Such a display of mercy is strictly done out of sense of reluctant obligation or self-righteousness. However, with the pure quality of tenderness surrounding it, mercy becomes the out-flowing of God's kind of love, straight from the heart. It displays the heart of Christ. Clothe your acts of mercy with tenderness of heart.

## Kindness

The biblical use of the word *"kindness"* carries the idea of excellence of moral character. It describes an approach to mercy as a gentle, compassionate, healing process. It stands on the solid ground of the integrity of a man's heart. Its strength is in its gentleness. Clothe your acts of mercy with deliberate kindness.

## Humility

The meanings of the word *"humility"* could fill a book by themselves. Every Samswim needs to think of himself in terms of swimming through shark territory with a modest, grateful attitude. Jesus did not consider it robbery with God to take His rightful, exalted place at the right hand of the Father. Yet, He humbled Himself, even to death on the cross, so we could safely swim through the sharks. We claim our destinies, clothed with the same kind of humility.

## Gentleness
### (*"meekness"* in the KJV and NKJV versions)

Though each is a different word in its original Greek use, *"gentleness,"* and *"meekness"* are closely related to *"humility."* The idea of gentleness repeats the earlier thought of Colossians 3:12, emphasizing the impact of a humble disposition. I have heard it said that meekness is not weakness. To the contrary, meekness is a source of strength. Clothe yourself in gentle meekness.

## Patience

Patience is not a natural trait in any of us. You acquire *"patience"* through effort and practice. It is a sacrificial act that says, *I will wait for God's best as I subject my pride and desires to His will and His ways.* Patience requires you to allow God's timing to have dominion over the direction and pace of your life. Purpose is always fulfilled through patience. Clothe yourself in *"patience."* Then, pursue your purpose until you have it in your grasp.

Once you have clothed yourselves with tenderhearted mercy, kindness, humility, gentleness, and patience, you are properly dressed for a safe swim.

# Swimming Instructions

*(Colossians 3:15-17 NLT) "And let the peace that comes from Christ rule in your hearts. For as members of one body you are all called to live in peace. And always be thankful. {16} Let the words of Christ, in all their richness, live in your hearts and make you wise. Use his words to teach and counsel each other. Sing psalms and hymns and spiritual songs to God with*

*thankful hearts. {17} And whatever you do or say, let it be as a representative of the Lord Jesus, all the while giving thanks through him to God the Father."*

Surrender your heart to the peace of God. Honor the words of Christ. Let them come alive in your life. They will be the foundations to support His peace as it works in you. When you do, you will be giving God's Word an abiding, permanent and comfortable home within you. Make it your habit that all you do or say, is in the name of Christ, and filled with thanksgiving to God.

When you align yourself with God's swimming instructions from Colossians 3:15-17, you will experience the power found in God's protecting presence. Strive to limit your participation in activities that will hook and capture you for shark bait. Seek His will. Find and press into it. You will draw closer to Him, fully protected and well able to perform His will. Do so now, even as you are reading this. He will draw near to you.

*(James 4:8a NKJV) "Draw near to God and He will draw near to you."*

Navigate the currents of your life with all these instructions and you will neither be shark bait, nor ride the morality slide. You will be more than a conqueror by faith in Him who is able to do exceedingly, abundantly far above whatever you might ask or think. You will be God's winner and champion.

*(Ephesians 3:20-21 NKJV) "Now to Him who is able to do exceedingly abundantly above all that we ask or think, according to the power that works in us, {21} to Him be glory in the church by Christ Jesus to all generations, forever and ever. Amen."*

Do not be a wimp.                          Be a winner!

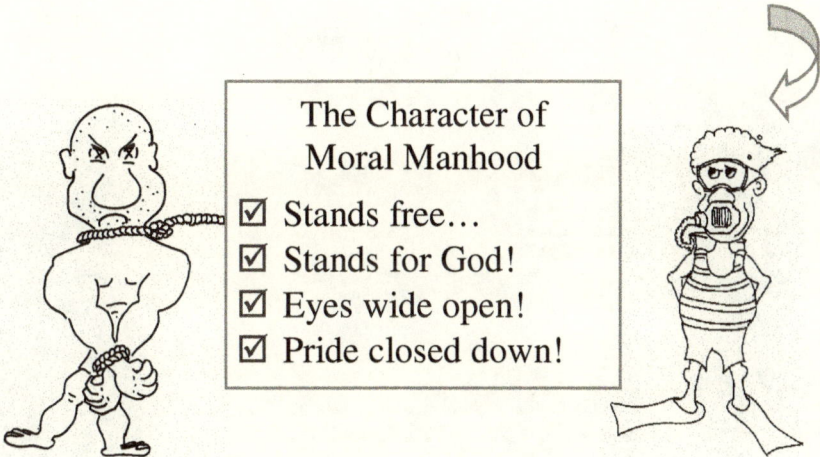

The Character of
Moral Manhood

☑ Stands free…
☑ Stands for God!
☑ Eyes wide open!
☑ Pride closed down!

# Chapter 3

# Hooked on Compassion

## - How You Look at Others -

### (Understanding the value of the people God has given you to love and care for)

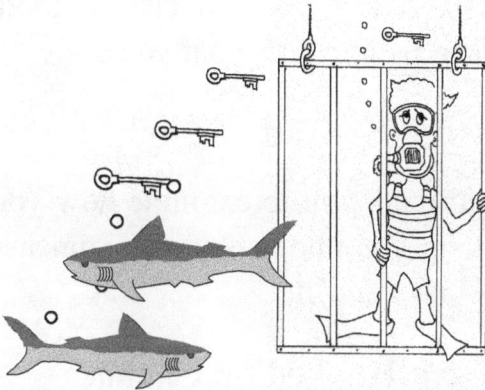

In the two earlier chapters, you learned about the protective places God provides within your own manhood. You saw that these were formed from your humility and other dependable components. The shark cage also comes with a locked gate. You will need to access the gate, when you are in need of safety. As you know, it takes a key to open a locked gate. This chapter and the three that follow will call your attention to four vital keys of moral manhood. God, in His loving provision, provides a moral man with these four unique keys. They will fit the locked gate of your shark cage in every circumstance or situation. Here are the keys.

## Key #1: Hooked on Compassion

This first key explores how a moral man looks at others. It asks you to consider the value of the people God has given you to love and care for.

## Key #2: Hooked on Holiness

This second key emphasizes the value of progressive personal holiness. It asks you to take a good look inside yourself and understand what you see.

## Key #3: Hooked on God

This third key prompts you to examine how you look at God. It will help you understand the immeasurable value He brings into your life.

## Key #4: Hooked on Change

Change is inevitable. This final key helps you understand the value of change in your life and in the lives of those around you.

Let's go to your first key.

# Key #1: Hooked on Compassion

## - How you look at others -

(Understanding the value of the people God has given you to love and care for)

God purposely positions people in your life for you to love and care for. They are as vital to your purpose as you are to theirs. Your willingness to esteem and care for them will insulate you from the dangers of being too self-centered or selfish. Are you letting pride or anything else prevent you from cherishing and valuing family, friends, and the people God has given you to love and care for? If so, you are inviting strong limitations to rule your life, blind your judgment and distort your discernment. You are swimming in dangerous waters.

There will always be circumstances and distractions aimed at diverting you from your responsibilities toward others. They are lurking like sharks, waiting to chase you from the God-ordained course of your life. These distractions will put a bite on your dreams, ambitions and opportunities.

Who or what is there that distracts you from being a man of compassion, like our friend, Samswim? What might draw you toward having an uncaring attitude and becoming a little bit more like Samson? He was enticed to disregard the well-being of others for his own selfish reasons.

At the end of his life, Samson sorrowed over his loss of the eternal perspective with which he began. He mourned that he had not done things differently.

Your survival and success are keyed to having your priorities in order. Among the greatest of your priorities must be a commitment to place the highest value on those God gives you to love and care for. Protecting this priority will influence your daily-decision making processes so they are beneficial to them.

Look into the mirror of your soul and ask yourself these questions.

- Do your choices always affect and influence those you love and care for in a positive way?
- Do too many of your decisions result in unexpected, negative outcomes for others?
- Do your decisions drive others away from God's divine covering and blessings?

Moral manhood requires that you consider the welfare of others before you act. If your actions consistently influence others in negative ways, you have the power to reverse this. Within you is the ability to influence the people in your world in positive ways. This requires you to have an attitude of compassion, so you can touch them and make a difference.

Consider this carefully. If you will value those God has given you to love and care for, the limits on your manhood and life will wash away. Satisfaction, success and significance will become companions on your journey to your destiny.

Think of what a difference you can make in the lives of those you love and care for. Do not waste an opportunity for them to be thankful that you are a part of their lives. Do what is right in the sight of the Lord. Be a moral man of God and make a difference. Then, as you look into that mirror of your soul, you will like what you see.

## Boaz

*(Ruth 2:4 NKJV) "Now behold, Boaz came from Bethlehem, and said to the reapers, "The LORD be with you!" And they answered him, "The LORD bless you!""*

Boaz and those who worked under his authority valued each other. Boaz desired God's blessings for them, and genuinely wished them well. He conducted himself as an honorable man in his dealings toward the people he held power over.

Relationships are invaluable. They are not something easily replaced. Boaz saw his men as valuable in God's sight and therefore, valuable to him. They, in turn, respected him and worked well for him. One thing is obvious. Boaz's conduct as a leader, landowner and businessman had a positive effect on those who relied upon him for their well-being. The character of his moral manhood included kindness and appreciation for the value of his people.

---

### LIFELINE
Your attitude about others in your care directly affects your successes in life.

---

*(Ruth 2:8-9 NKJV) "Then Boaz said to Ruth, "You will listen, my daughter, will you not? Do not go to glean in another field, nor go from here, but stay close by my young women. {9} Let your eyes be on the field which they reap, and go after them. Have I not commanded the young men not to touch you? And when you are thirsty, go to the vessels and drink from what the young men have drawn.""*

Boaz could have played the shark. He had the power to deny Ruth access to the field. He could have tried to coerce her into doing anything to get the grain. He could have taken advantage of her physically and emotionally. However, Boaz's actions toward Ruth in that field demonstrated his commitment to moral manhood. He knew she was vulnerable. At that moment, he chose to respect, protect and provide for her. The character of moral manhood is to show mercy and restraint of power, when it is tempting to use it against others (especially those who are most vulnerable).

---

### LIFELINE

Your attitude about those who are vulnerable to you directly affects their lives and well-being.

---

*(Ruth 2:10-12 NKJV) "So she fell on her face, bowed down to the ground, and said to him, "Why have I found favor in your eyes, that you should take notice of me, since I am a foreigner?" {11} And Boaz answered and said to her, "It has been fully reported to me, all that you have done for your mother-in-law since the death of your husband, and how you have left your father and your mother and the land of your birth, and have come to a people whom you did not know before. {12} The LORD repay your work, and a full reward be given you by the LORD God of Israel, under whose wings you have come for refuge.""*

A life of moral manhood requires you to have a compassionate awareness of others around you. It does not allow you to live in isolation, concerned only with your needs. You never have a valid excuse to disregard the needs of other people. God expects that you will actively seek to contribute to the welfare of others. A godly man of moral character consistently looks for ways to open doors of opportunity for the less fortunate.

I believe that the single best definition of a man's leadership is "influence." Boaz had great influence on Ruth's life and the lives of so many others. Moral manhood does not limit others to gleaning leftovers. Because of your demonstration of godly influence, they can gain a full supply. Ask yourself what it is that motivates your life and ministry to those around you. What kind of influence are you on those you lead? Are you hooked on compassion for those around you whom God has given you to love and care for?

> LIFELINE
> Sow seeds motivated by your love. You will reap a full harvest motivated by God's love.

*(Ruth 2:13-16 NKJV) "Then she said, "Let me find favor in your sight, my lord; for you have comforted me, and have spoken kindly to your maidservant, though I am not like one of your*

*maidservants." {14} Now Boaz said to her at mealtime, "Come here, and eat of the bread, and dip your piece of bread in the vinegar." So she sat beside the reapers, and he passed parched grain to her; and she ate and was satisfied, and kept some back. {15} And when she rose up to glean, Boaz commanded his young men, saying, "Let her glean even among the sheaves, and do not reproach her. {16} Also let grain from the bundles fall purposely for her; leave it that she may glean, and do not rebuke her.""*

Boaz was more than just a source of comfort and kindness. He was a deliberate and determined source of God's increase for others. Ruth got more than scraps from the field. She got bundles of grain that were left purposely in her path. The character of moral manhood is to be a deliberate instrument of increase for others, regardless of the personal cost.

Do you have handfuls of abundant purpose that brings those around you God's blessings? Do not allow them to settle for gleaning leftovers. Do not allow moral limitations to keep you and those around you from an abundant life.

---

### LIFELINE
Be a reflection of Jesus. Humble yourself and give of yourself without regard to personal cost.

---

Boaz's humble character motivated his behavior toward others. It empowered him to be a positive influence on those his life touched. All he was and all he did reflected God's character, at work in him. The character of a moral man is the character of Christ.

*(Ruth 3:8-9 NKJV) "Now it happened at midnight that the man was startled, and turned himself; and there, a woman was lying at his feet. {9} And he said, "Who are you?" So she answered, "I am Ruth, your maidservant. Take your maidservant under your wing, for you are a close relative.""*

During the harvest, Boaz slept with his men on the threshing floor. It had been a hard day's work. Suddenly at midnight, he awoke in the darkness to find Ruth at his feet. He asked, *"Who are you?"* She replied, *"I am Ruth, your maidservant. Take your maidservant under your wing, for you are a near kinsman."*

When confronted with what could have been strong temptation, Boaz was a man of godly reaction. He was a man who could be trusted to have control over his temptations. Ruth said, *"Take me under your wing."* She knew she was safe in his hands.

Are you answering God's call to be a safe harbor for others who face personal peril, uncertainty or even storms?

## Staying on a Course of Compassion

*(1 Corinthians 11:1 NKJV) "Imitate me, just as I also imitate Christ."*

Where is your compassion at right now? Who do you imitate most of the time? Are you joining with God, imitating Him and loving like Him 100% of the time? Is it more like 90% of the time? ...85%? ...80%? ...50%? In which of these percentages does your level of compassion fit? The gap between where you fit and 100% may seem inconsequential, but it indicates there is the potential to drive you well off your course (out of the shark cage), as you go through life. Do you need a heart adjustment?

I heard a great illustration of a man whose course was off the mark. I do not remember its source, and cannot credit whoever originated it, but it is worth telling. As you read it, let it speak to your soul.

> There was a commander in the Royal Navy who was very independent and proud. He worked his way through the ranks and always seemed to come out on top. Finally, he became the captain of a mighty warship with huge, magnificent guns. It was the pride of the British fleet.
>
> One dark stormy night the captain was on the bridge when he spotted a light in the distance. It was rapidly closing with the warship and

49

seemed to be on a collision course. As his huge ship rose and fell in the waves of the storm, he watched the light getting closer. He ordered his signalman to flash this message to the unidentified light, *"Alter your course ten degrees to the south."*

Within seconds the reply came back, *"Alter your course ten degrees to the north."* Determined that his ship would never take second place to another, he snapped an order to the signalman. Tell them this, *"Alter your course ten degrees to the south. I am the captain of the Battleship Endeavor!"* The response came back again, *"Alter your course ten degrees to the north; I am Seaman Third class Smith."* By this time, the light was becoming ever brighter and larger. Infuriated, the captain grabbed the signal light and personally signaled, *"Alter your course, I am a battleship!"* The reply came back just as quickly, *"Alter your course, I am a lighthouse."*

We can easily find ourselves missing signals that would keep us on course. As we saw with Boaz, a moral man maintains a course of compassion. He is aware of those things that would shipwreck his integrity and bring hurt to those he loves and cares for. Being filled with the compassion of Christ is the first key to moral manhood. It will allow you to see the light and avoid the rocks. The people God has given you are not meant to be shipwrecked or shark bitten… and neither are you.

---

### LIFELINE

Do not settle for less than 100% of the character of God in your life. Make every course adjustment He commands.

---

# Chapter 4

# Key #2: Hooked on Holiness

## - How you look at yourself -

## (Understanding the value of progressive personal holiness)

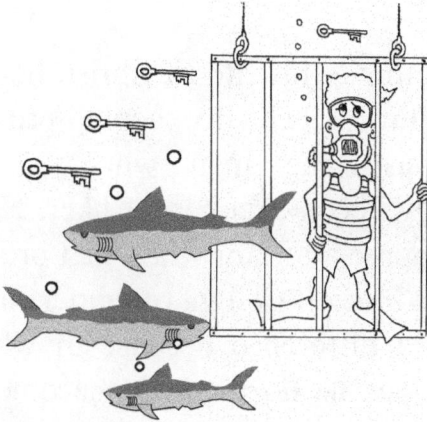

In this chapter, we will navigate the waters of the second key to moral manhood, being hooked on holiness.

## Why is personal holiness so important?

*(Ephesians 1:4 NKJV) "just as He chose us in Him before the foundation of the world, that we should be holy and without blame before Him in love,"*

Even before you knew Him, God chose you to be holy and without blame. He made this possible through the substitutionary atonement of Christ. As a Christian man, you are now positioned to live a life that honors and pleases God. He is watching. He is rooting for you. He desires that you become all you can be. To help you do that, He has given you a command to pursue holiness.

> *(Hebrews 12:14 NKJV) "Pursue peace with all people, and holiness, without which no one will see the Lord."*

When a man commits his life to Christ, he discovers an urgency within his heart to become progressively more like Jesus. The man who was once a heartbreaker now becomes a peacemaker. He is filled with thankful appreciation for what the Lord has done for him. He sees himself in light of who he now is and wants to make a difference because of who he has become. How does he do that? He becomes hooked on holiness. The following verse of Scripture is clear. Read it carefully.

> *(1 Peter 1:15-16 NKJV) "but as He who called you is holy, you also be holy in all your conduct, {16} because it is written, "Be holy, for I am holy.""*

Peter's words are more than an invitation. They are a biblical command to be holy. Make no mistake. God does not consider

holiness optional. Obedience to this command brings a harvest of eternal blessings. A foundational truth for your life is that the only way God can work with you and for you is if He can work in you. He will not force his way upon you. Compliance will be your decision. What will it be, holiness and blessings... or something else? When you choose holiness, you embrace the opportunities of moral manhood.

*(1 Corinthians 11:28a NKJV) "But let a man examine himself..."*

## Holiness is...

Pursuing holiness requires the determined removal of sinful negatives, replacing them with biblical positives. This gives Christ indisputable first place in every area of your life. As you do this, you will find you are giving the devil, the world and the flesh no place to influence or operate within you. This is the process we call sanctification.

*(1 Thessalonians 4:1-8 NKJV) "Finally then, brethren, we urge and exhort in the Lord Jesus that you should abound more and more, just as you received from us how you ought to walk and to please God; {2} for you know what commandments we gave you through the Lord Jesus. {3} For this is the will of God, your sanctification: that you should abstain from sexual immorality; {4} that each of you should*

*know how to possess his own vessel in sanctification and honor, {5} not in passion of lust, like the Gentiles who do not know God; {6} that no one should take advantage of and defraud his brother in this matter, because the Lord is the avenger of all such, as we also forewarned you and testified. {7} For God did not call us to uncleanness, but in holiness. {8} Therefore he who rejects this does not reject man, but God, who has also given us His Holy Spirit."*

Paul's words clearly establish the will of God, which is our sanctification. To be sanctified is to be separated *from* evil and set apart *to* God. This is a continuous process, which takes us progressively closer to Christ. It leads us to realize our potential as men of God. Paul is specific in his explanation of what should be among a moral man's highest priorities. He teaches us to honor our bodies, keeping them free of sexual immorality and lust. Then Paul moves on to the requirement that we honor the character of Christ within us. We are to display it as a testimony to our commitment.

The sanctification Paul writes about is only possible because of God's grace. We need God's help. We cannot sanctify ourselves. Our responsibility then, is to surrender every area of our lives to His Lordship. In our submission and surrender, we cooperate with His grace, letting it shape our hearts, step-by-step. This results in progressively become the uncompromising moral men He called us to be.

There are two conditions for sanctification. First, you must have faith in Jesus Christ as Lord and Savior. (If you have never done this, right now, you can ask Jesus to forgive you of your sins and come into your heart.) Second, you must be willing to change, hungering to become the man of God you have the potential to be. The possibilities are limitless.

Every moral man's challenge is that he *"should know how to possess his own vessel in sanctification and honor..."* Real men separate themselves from the pack. They value, to the extreme, their commitment to be honorable. They refuse to be enslaved by ungodly passions and lusts. Lust and ungodly passion can be for many things, including money, possessions, position, power or fame. Understand the value of your own holiness. Samswim decided to be passionate about that for which God was passionate. He established biblical controls over his thinking and therefore, his actions. He was hooked on holiness.

Being hooked on holiness is being securely captured by a burning desire within, to be completely devoted to God. It is commitment to a lifestyle that refuses to compromise your character. A holy life is tied to holy behavior. If you want to test how much of a holy God lives in you, ask yourself how much of Him shines forth out of you.

*(Matthew 5:14-16 NKJV) "You are the light of the world. A city that is set on a hill cannot be hidden. {15} Nor do they light a lamp and put it under a basket, but on a lampstand, and it gives light to all who are in the house. {16} Let your light so shine before men, that they may see your good works and glorify your Father in heaven."*

Personal holiness is a fraud, and you are fooling yourself... unless it affects others around you. If your holiness remains self-focused, you become like the priest in the Parable of the Good Samaritan, who ignored the wounded man.

*(Luke 10:30-31, 33-34 NKJV) "Then Jesus answered and said: "A certain man went down from Jerusalem to Jericho, and fell among thieves, who stripped him of his clothing, wounded him, and departed, leaving him half dead. {31} Now by chance a certain priest came down that road. And when he saw him, he passed by on the other side... {33} But a certain Samaritan, as he journeyed, came where he was. And when he saw him, he had compassion. {34} So he went to him and bandaged his wounds, pouring on oil and wine; and he set him on his own animal, brought him to an inn, and took care of him."*

God did not call you to walk on the other side of someone's trouble. You are God's champion. Make a difference for people who cannot help themselves. Chumps hide from this opportunity. They become shark bait. You are not a chump. You are a champ. Embrace your opportunity.

> LIFELINE
> Your holiness is personal, but its test of authenticity is completely interpersonal.

Do not forget our friend Samson's story. He had blinded himself to an eternal perspective. How he must have wished he had done things differently. His life was wasted. His end was defined by lost opportunity. He mourned his utter disregard for holiness before the Lord.

Personal holiness is not a buffet luncheon where you pick what you like and leave what might not taste so good. Personal holiness is a feast that fills you with abundant life. Leave nothing on the table that the Master serves you. Look again at Paul's words to the church at Thessalonica.

*(1 Thessalonians 4:7 NKJV) "For God did not call us to uncleanness, but in holiness."*

To reject a holy life is to reject God Himself. When you understand the value of progressive personal holiness, you will keep your spiritual eyes and ears wide open. You will seek to find where you might be resisting even a tiny bit of God's presence or His influence in your life. Again, leave nothing on the table that the Master serves you.

---

**LIFELINE**
Personal holiness requires that you resist any attraction to, or tolerance for, the unholy.

---

Holiness is a personal choice that is sourced from within. When you allow God to have dominion in your heart, He honors your decision for holiness. He abides in you so He can share your life. Remember, He does not wish to share His space with anything that offends Him. The Bible says, in 1 Corinthians 11:28, that you are to examine yourself before coming to the table with Christ. Reject whatever you find within your heart that offends Him. Reject those things that are not pleasing to Him. Communion with Christ is more than an ordinance of the church to be practiced on certain occasions. For every moral man, it ought to be continual and constant.

God knows that rejection of the unholy is a progressive process. In His boundless grace, He gives imperfect men His perfect presence within. The amazing thing is that He chooses to do this in spite of what He finds in us. Only God's kind of love makes this possible. You are highly favored. You are positioned to see God's presence increase your spiritual maturity, as you submit to Him. Doing so allows you to become progressively more in touch with Him and more like Him. In time, the things that offend His holiness are driven out of your life. You can look forward to this sanctification process, knowing He freely gives it.

Be quick to recognize when God places a meaningful moment in front of you. This is a moment when a particular truth becomes the tool of transformation to bring you closer to personal holiness. Fully and quickly embrace every attraction to the things of God. Feel the tug at your heart and react to it. Remember, the only way God can work with you and for you is if He can work in you.

---

**LIFELINE**
Personal holiness grows as you
embrace a hunger for change - daily,
hourly and minute-by-minute.

---

Let your hunger for transformation fan the flames of holiness, so it burns like a fire within you. You should have the highest expectation that this day you will take another step, cross another bridge, climb another mountain and walk a narrower path. You will do whatever it takes to ignite something new and brighter inside. Personal holiness will only come with your expectation and desire to be transformed. Let there be a burning in your heart for Jesus. Make this your daily confession.

*God, help me to understand the value of progressive personal holiness and to cause it to burn within my heart!*

## Wisdom for a Moral Man

The Apostle Paul's writings provide every man with a clear wakeup call not to be like Samson. They are a warning to keep a watch for those sharks that so easily prey on your carnality, desiring to devour your commitment to holiness before the Lord.

*(Ephesians 5:6-7 NKJV) "Let no one deceive you with empty words, for because of these things the wrath of God comes upon the sons of disobedience. {7} Therefore do not be partakers with them."*

As we have seen, Delilah's deceptive words enticed Samson's heart. He paid the ultimate price. He lost his manhood and became a slave, chained to a pillar. Samson's sinfully wrong thinking was, *I am*

*invincible in my own strength.* He should have rejected the advances of this evil, enticing woman. He should have turned to his dependence on God. Had he done so, he would have been remembered for all those years He faithfully judged Israel. Instead, his legacy was nothing more than crumbling pillars and a painfully sad ending. A moral man knows the value of progressive personal holiness. When temptation comes, he searches within and finds the holiness that will protect his heart. Then, he clings to it.

> *(James 1:12, 16-17 NKJV) "Blessed is the man who endures temptation; for when he has been approved, he will receive the crown of life which the Lord has promised to those who love Him... Do not be deceived, my beloved brethren. {17} Every good gift and every perfect gift is from above, and comes down from the Father of lights, with whom there is no variation or shadow of turning."*

> *(Ephesians 5:8-11 NKJV) "For you were once darkness, but now you are light in the Lord. Walk as children of light {9} (for the fruit of the Spirit is in all goodness, righteousness, and truth), {10} finding out what is acceptable to the Lord. {11} And have no fellowship with the unfruitful works of darkness, but rather expose them."*

Christ will walk in the light with you. His presence will illuminate your path so it shines ever brighter. A man of God receives and embraces the light.

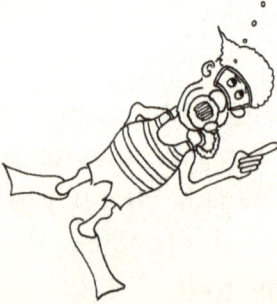

*(Proverbs 4:18-19 NKJV)*
*"But the path of the just is like the shining sun, That shines ever brighter unto the perfect day."*

It should become apparent that Keys #1 and #2 are meant to work together to unlock the mysteries of Christian success. Man up! Get hooked! Love the people God gives you. Embrace a moral man's ways of progressive personal holiness. Take these two keys and open some gates with them. You will watch the sharks swim by, and never be their bait, because you will never be a chump. You will always be a champ - a winner and a champion for Jesus!

# Chapter 5

# Key #3: Hooked on God

## - How you look at God -

### (Understanding the value of knowing who God is)

In this chapter, we will navigate the waters of your third key to moral manhood, being "Hooked on God." The focus of the first key, "Understanding the value of the people God has given you to love and care for," was about what you see when you look at others. The focus of the second key, "Understanding the value of progressive personal holiness," was about what you see when you look at yourself. The focus of this chapter (the third key), "Understanding the value of knowing who God is," will be about what you see when you look at God.

Whether you are looking at others, yourself or God, what you see will be determined by the lens through which you look. For every man, this lens is shaped by his experiences, opinions, education, prejudices and most importantly, whether or not he has surrendered himself to the Lord. You will only have an accurate view of yourself and others when you can see God for who He really is.

# Looking at Your Manhood by
# Looking to God

Through what kind of lens do you see God? To understand the value of knowing who God is, you must clearly see what Scripture reveals about Him. The Word of God will be your distortion-free lens through which to see Him. Your proper view of the Lord will determine your understanding of your own manhood, and consequently, the quality, influence and impact of your life.

# Who is God?

In New Testament Scripture, there are four direct statements of who God is. Each gives a moral man of God absolute assurance for his journey through life. Together, these four statements leave no doubt. They are short, concise declarations of His absolute authority, wisdom and power. They speak of the completeness of God and His provision.

1. *"God is light."* (1 John 1:5)
2. *"God is love."* (1 John 4:8, 16)
3. *"God is Spirit."* (John 4:24)
4. *"God is a consuming fire."* (Hebrews 12:29)

These four statements display the enormity of God's glory. They are your assurance that this awesome God who loves you is always with you. They guarantee you will have a sure foundation for kingdom living. The man of God who believes what God says about

Himself will discover the meaning of our third key. "Understanding the value of knowing who God is" will illuminate the path to your destiny. You will see your dreams fulfilled. What you reach for is what you will get. With God all things are possible and nothing is impossible... as long as you understand Him accurately through the lens of Scripture. Let's look at these four basic descriptions of God in the New Testament.

# 1. God is Light

*(1 John 1:5 NKJV) "This is the message which we have heard from Him and declare to you, that God is light and in Him is no darkness at all."*

## Wisdom for Champions

When we think of darkness, it brings to mind the unknown. When faced with the unknown, and all its blinding uncertainty and confusion, even the strongest man could succumb to it. The only sure remedy for the darkness of the unknown is to have with you the unfailing source of completely dependable, divine illumination. 1 John 1:5 tells us, *"God is light."* When God is with you, you may experience the approach of darkness, but the darkness has no choice but to flee from His presence. This principle never varies. When light comes, darkness flees. Walk with God and you walk in the light of this divine guarantee. As you exercise your faith, the uncertainty of facing the unknown will flee. When you have God, you are assured of overcoming whatever casts dark shadows on you.

God is more than a divine illumination source. He is the "light of the world." Men who follow Christ, walk with the light of victory in their hearts. Their paths and their confidence are enlightened by His presence. Have you seen God for who He is, in all His glory?

> *(John 8:12 NKJV) "Then Jesus spoke to them again, saying, "I am the light of the world. He who follows Me shall not walk in darkness, but have the light of life."*

Dr. Charles Stanley is a great man of God. I once heard him tell about his early days, pastoring his first church. Let his story speak to your heart.

> At the time, young Pastor Stanley was going through an unpleasant, difficult time. The church he pastored was troubled and divided. Some wanted him to remain as their pastor and others wanted him to resign.

> A very old woman, who was a member of the congregation, approached him at the end of the service and asked him to come to lunch at her home. There was something that she wanted to show him. He agreed, and after church ended for the day, they went to her home. When they arrived, he was about to sit down, but she asked him to come over to the wall of her living room

and look at a picture. As he did, he saw it was a painting of Daniel in the Lions' Den. *"What do you see?"* asked the old woman. *"Tell me everything you see in the painting."*

Pastor Stanley began to describe what he saw in the painting. *"It is dark in the lions' den. Some lions are sleeping. Others have their eyes on Daniel. There are bones everywhere. There is a bright light in the image of a man in one part of the lion's den."*

*"What else do you see?"* she asked. *"That is all I see."* Pastor Stanley replied. *"You missed the most important thing,"* she said. *"Look at Daniel's eyes. They are fixed on the light!"*

*"They are fixed on the light!"*

Here is the formula for a successful, significant, God-pleasing life. Fix your spiritual eyes on the light. God is the light. Light defeats darkness and brings you the provision of awareness. Awareness leads to wisdom. Wisdom is the foundation of a sure walk and a victorious life.

## 2. God is Love

God does so much more than illuminate our journeys through life with His presence. He also empowers our journeys with the most powerful gift any man could receive and subsequently give, His kind of love.

*(1 John 4:8 NKJV) "He who does not love does not know God, for God is love."*

*(1 John 4:16b, 18-19 NKJV) "...God is love, and he who abides in love abides in God, and God in him... {18} There is no fear in love; but perfect love casts out fear, because fear involves torment. But he who fears has not been made perfect (complete) in love. {19} We love Him because He first loved us."*

God's kind of love has the power to melt a man's icy heart. It takes it from being cold, hardened, brittle, and fearful - to soft, warm, pliable and filled with faith. God brings His love into the hearts of men who believe in and commit to following Him. His abiding love has the power to drive out, cancel, obliterate, and make of absolutely no consequence the fears that so desperately want to darken our lives. The issue is not whether fear wants to leave, but that with God's love in action, it has no choice. Fear no longer has a voice. It must go. His love carries the guarantee that, when given a home in a man's heart, it will drive out fear. This principle becomes our next LIFELINE.

> **LIFELINE**
> God's perfect love drives out and
> utterly obliterates fear.

## God's Kind of Love

Consider my definition for God's kind of love.

*God's kind of love is your deliberate, active, living effort to bring to someone, as much of God's grace as possible, at whatever the cost to you.*

Only God's kind of love releases the flow of God's grace. Generally speaking, grace is defined as God's unmerited favor. It cannot be earned. It is a gift. Without a clear, accurate understanding of what God's grace is, your grasp of God's kind of love will be incomplete. His grace and love cannot be separated. They go hand-in-hand. Consider my definition of grace.

*Grace is the goodness of God, stored up in heaven, just waiting for your willingness to allow it to flow through you to someone else.*

Your willingness to allow God's grace to flow through you is a demonstration of real love - God's kind of love.

God will move sovereignly as He chooses. However, most of the time, His grace flows through people. When a moral man of God is willing, he becomes a conduit for, or dispenser of God's grace. Willing moral men are championship grace dispensers.

When you understand and embrace the power of the gift of grace, shown through God's kind of love, you will have divine assurance that you can swim through the sharks of life. If you will make room for His kind of love in your heart, and bring His grace to others, you can trust Him to be in complete control. With God's kind of love at work in you, everything will be all right.

> **LIFELINE**
> Release God's grace from within you and it will drive away the sharks from around you.

# 3. God is Spirit

*(John 4:23-24 NKJV) "But the hour is coming, and now is, when the true worshipers will worship the Father in spirit and truth; for the Father is seeking such to worship Him. {24} God is Spirit, and those who worship Him must worship in spirit and truth."*

In this Gospel narrative, Jesus clearly said that God is not a material being. He is a divine, ever-present Spirit Being. God is infinitely bigger than a man's thinking can grasp. He is everything He says He is, and will do everything He says He will do. Every Samswim learns to trust the Lord with all of his heart.

When necessary, he puts his brain in neutral and simply trusts. Trust invites God's power. Trust acknowledges that God is omnipresent from the highest mountain to the depths of the deepest sea. A moral man looks to God in the spirit.

*(Proverbs 3:5 NKJV) "Trust in the LORD with all your heart, And lean not on your own understanding."*

Psalm 139: A Great Picture of God's Omnipresence.

*(Psalm 139:7-12 NKJV) "Where can I go from Your Spirit? Or where can I flee from Your presence? {8} If I ascend into heaven, You are there; If I make my bed in hell, behold, You are there. {9} If I take the wings of the morning, And dwell in the uttermost parts of the sea, {10} Even there Your hand shall lead me, And Your right hand shall hold me. {11} If I say, "Surely the darkness shall fall on me," Even the night shall be light about me; {12} Indeed, the darkness shall not hide from You, But the night shines as the day; The darkness and the light are both alike to You."*

Every man who faithfully follows God has the divine assurance that anywhere he goes, God goes with him. Regardless of whether you find yourself in a good, bad or ugly place, God is always there. He said He would never leave you nor forsake you. God loves you so much that you cannot shake Him, even if you try to hide from Him or turn from Him. Do you sense Him in the midst of every moment of your life? If not, ask yourself, why not? The answer will be found within you.

## 4. God is a Consuming Fire

*(Hebrews 12:29 NKJV) "For our God is a consuming fire."*

Nothing escapes a consuming fire. When fire-fighters and their equipment come too close to a consuming fire, they are simply burned up from the intense heat. Likewise, the fire of God springs into action to overwhelm, trap and consume what dares to confront Him or His servants. When God ignites it, His power is devastating. Nothing can quench it.

We have previously looked at the challenges a man's pride and self-dependence bring, with their inevitably negative consequences. The lesson of God as *"a consuming fire"* is basic. He is neither to be taken for granted, nor forgotten. He is Lord and Savior. He is the source of everything good. God's omnipotence (His authority, power and might) is beyond challenge

74

and His wrath is all-consuming. The best part of all this is that when you have given your life to Him, He is on your side. If God is for you, who could be successfully against you?

> *(Romans 8:31 NKJV) "What then shall we say to these things? If God is for us, who can be against us?"*

As you commit to a life of moral manhood, you position yourself to enjoy the protection of God's amazing power. You are fireproof! When the sharks threaten to attack, you have the safety of the divine shark cage. It gives you a front row seat to watch the consuming fire of God defend you.

## Another Perspective on a Consuming Fire

God's consuming fire can also burn out of you all that displeases Him. Welcome that holy fire into your heart. Fan the flames of desperation to become more like Him. When you embrace this desperation, you become dangerous to the devil and your fiery faith in action will glorify God.

---

### LIFELINE
God is completely dependable, and fully able to consume what tries to consume you.

---

75

This chapter began with the principle that what you see will be determined by the lens through which you look. I have presented you with an unclouded, distortion-free lens that shows God is light, love, Spirit and a consuming fire. Seeing these truths will help you grasp how precious and vital it is to understand the value of knowing who God is. Apply this third key to your life and watch it ignite your faith. Let it define the set of your sail. Then the winds of the Spirit will set heaven in motion and take you to your destiny.

# Chapter 6

# Key #4: Hooked on Change
## - How you look at life -

(Understanding the value of change in your life… and in the lives of those around you)

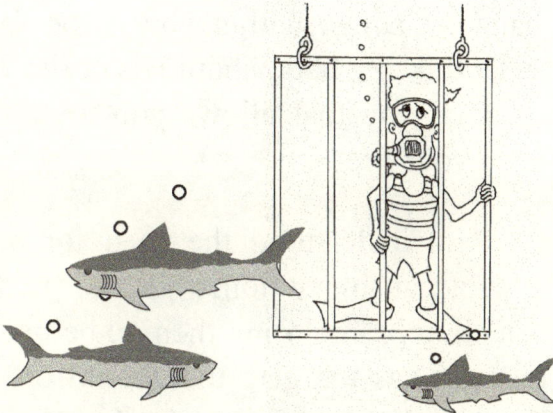

In this chapter, we will navigate the waters of the fourth key to moral manhood, being "Hooked on Change." Change comes in many ways. Sometimes it is beyond your control. It just happens "to" you, causing the conditions and circumstances around you to suddenly shift. To achieve a successful, significant, God-pleasing life, this kind of change will require your consistent willingness, and even eagerness, to adapt to the conditions in which you find yourself. Failure to acknowledge change, or fear to adapt to it, leads to a situation in which you become dead in the water, aimlessly floating here or there at the whim of unprincipled, unpredictable currents. Adaptability to change enables you to make the adjustments necessary to stay on course to your destiny.

How you handle the change that happens "to" you is greatly influenced by another type of change. This is the kind of change over which you do have control. It is change that happens "in" you - your own internal, personal change. Change within you is the focus of this chapter. God is emphatic about His desire for you to change in any way that allows you to fulfill His perfect will for your life.

The Apostle Paul understood the need for personal change. He wrote an impassioned plea to his friends in the Roman church, imploring them to be open to it. He knew change was the gate that would open their world to the best God had for them. Here is what he wrote.

> *(Romans 12:1-2 NKJV) "I beseech you therefore, brethren, by the mercies of God, that you present your bodies a living sacrifice, holy, acceptable to God, which is your reasonable service. {2} And do not be*

*conformed to this world, but be transformed by the renewing of your mind, that you may prove what is that good and acceptable and perfect will of God."*

Paul's letter to the Romans reveals the vital process needed for personal change. It illustrates the system a moral man is to follow to arrive at the place where he is able to give evidence of the *"perfect,"* or mature and complete will of God. This process is an exchange of conformity for transformation. Paul writes, *"And do not be conformed to this world, but be transformed by the renewing of your mind."* Let's look inside these two words, *"conformed"* and *"transformed."*

To be *"conformed"* to this world means to be like others, who practice the sinful systems of thought and action that influence the currents of culture and society. These sinful systems of thought are dictated by our inherent carnality.

To be *"transformed"* means to undergo a change in your nature and character. You no longer practice the sinful systems of the world. Now, you reflect Christ in your thoughts and actions.

Transformation happens when the quality or nature of something changes. The Apostle Paul says, *"be transformed."* He means to change from what you were to what you ought to be, a moral man who is pleasing to the Lord in every possible way. When you accepted Christ, the essential qualities of your spirit and soul were unleashed to become all God designed them to be. Change was initiated. God designed this change to be progressive and continual. We call this sanctification. It is vital to a man's transformation and growth. When the Apostle Paul wrote to the Romans, he encouraged them to change their old ways of thinking. These same writings invite every one of us to do the same. Here is how it works. Your thinking drives your actions, and they drive your success, significance and the direction of your destiny.

> *Romans 12:2 (GWT) "Don't become like the people of this world. Instead, change the way you think. Then you will always be able to determine what God really wants - what is good, pleasing, and perfect."*

> *2 Corinthians 3:18 (NKJV) "But we all, with unveiled face, beholding as in a mirror the glory of the Lord, are being transformed into the same image from glory to glory, just as by the Spirit of the Lord."*

Are you changing so that you become as much like Jesus as possible, building your life in a positive, progressive pattern (*"from glory to glory"*)? You cannot achieve this kind of change by natural means.

It is only *"by the Spirit of the Lord."* It is an inward process that becomes outwardly evident to everyone around you. This process affects you and influences those around you. It transforms the eventual outcomes of your circumstances so they align with the will of God.

## The Process of Change

Change has three facets to it. The first is to crucify your flesh; the second, to renew your mind; and the third, to feed your spirit. As these three facets of change work together, they reflect your decision to become all God destined you to be. Your willingness releases God's power into your circumstances and directs your paths. Crucified flesh, a renewed mind and a well-fed spirit do a great job of maintaining the environment of your shark cage. The following diagram illustrates the process of change.

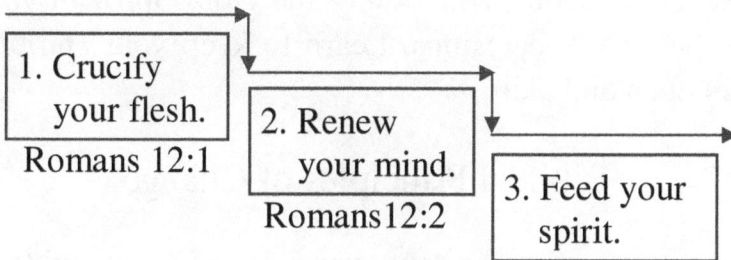

```
┌─────────────────┐
│ 1. Crucify      │──►
│    your flesh.  │   ┌─────────────────┐
└─────────────────┘   │ 2. Renew        │──►
  Romans 12:1         │    your mind.   │   ┌─────────────────┐
                      └─────────────────┘   │ 3. Feed your    │──►
                        Romans 12:2         │    spirit.      │
                                            └─────────────────┘
```

These work simultaneously, but it begins with the first facet, your daily decision to crucify your flesh (your sense of entitlement and independence).

*(Luke 9:23 NKJV) "Then He said to them all, "If anyone desires to come after Me, let him deny himself, and take up his cross daily, and follow Me."*

This denial of "self" sets things in motion. It requires daily effort, dedication and a mature understanding of the value of change. As you crucify your flesh, you form new attitudes and patterns of thinking. Doing this causes you to engage the second facet, renewing your mind. This must be a conscientious, deliberate part of your daily routine. It happens because you understand the value of change and work to make it happen. The third facet, happening at the same time, is that you are feeding your spirit. This will be greatly enhanced if you have a hunger to study God's Word and engage Him in communion and prayer. There are times you will set aside specifically for this, but consider making God your partner throughout the day. Get in the habit of involving the Holy Spirit in your smallest daily decisions. Learn to keep your spiritual ears open and alert.

## Biblical Principles of Change

I want to give you an overview of some biblical principles of change. They are inherent in God's plan for you to grow more resistant, and be able to overcome the sharks you face in your life. With these principles, you can refuse to become shark bait because you will not be hooked by sinful weakness. Watch the sharks swim the other way because your spirit shows up strong in the Lord, free from carnal thinking and all its limitations.

## First Principle of Change

What has not yet changed must be contained.
First, contain your thoughts.

All things concerning your carnal thinking and actions can be changed after they are contained. Never give them the freedom they want.

> *(2 Corinthians 10:3-5 NKJV) "For though we walk in the flesh, we do not war according to the flesh. {4} For the weapons of our warfare are not carnal but mighty in God for pulling down strongholds, {5} casting down arguments and every high thing that exalts itself against the knowledge of God, bringing every thought into captivity to the obedience of Christ,"*

The biggest obstacle every moral man faces is his own thinking. Your natural mind does not like to change. It has become comfortable within the limits of its present thinking. It does not like to rock the boat. As carnal men, we deliberately constrain our thoughts to old patterns. We model our next actions after our last actions. We can be reluctant to risk doing new or different things that our faith would demand. We limit the amount and quality of new thinking we will accept. This causes us to be resistant to allowing the Holy Spirit to teach us new applications of time honored biblical principles. This resistance stifles our creativity and denies us the opportunities within the changes we reject. The remedy is to contain those old thoughts and actions. Make room for Christ-centered thinking. Become hooked on change. Understand how valuable a gift it is.

## Second Principle of Change

Let the Holy Spirit lead you in every situation.

*(Romans 8:1 NKJV) "There is therefore now no condemnation to those who are in Christ Jesus, who do not walk according to the flesh, but according to the Spirit."*

Are you being led by the Spirit or the flesh?

*(1 John 2:16-17 NKJV) "For all that is in the world; the lust of the flesh, the lust of the eyes, and the pride of life; is not of the Father but is of the world. {17} And the world is passing away, and the lust of it; but he who does the will of God abides forever."*

See if this diagram has any place in your life.

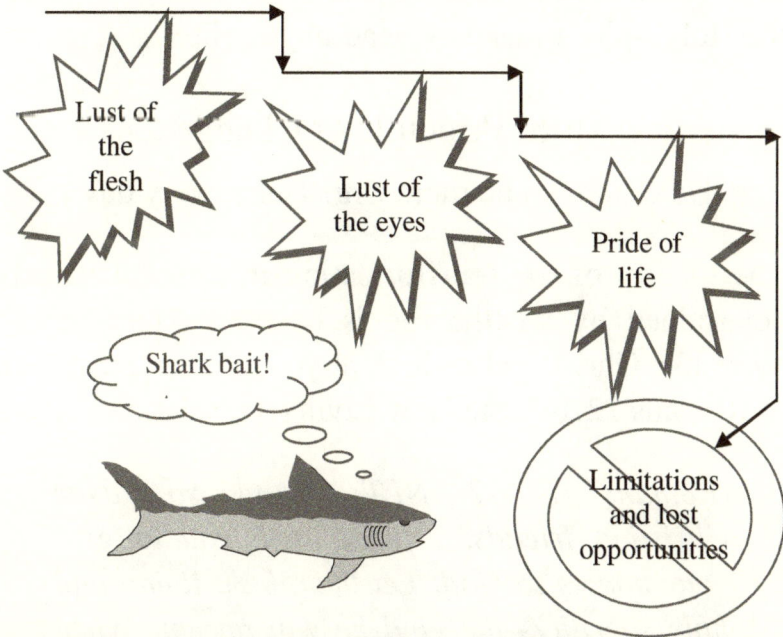

Are you walking with the Holy Spirit, or are you alone in an ocean of vulnerability and limitations? Does your day habitually include an awareness of what pleases God… and what displeases Him? Could you add something to the depths of your inner being that would free you from the shallows of worldly, lustful thinking, and take you into deeper waters?

Let us be honest. There are times when every man disconnects from his divine power source, the Spirit of God. Disconnecting from the Holy Spirit will freeze you into a sense of isolation in the situation in which you find yourself. If this happens, your opportunities for personal growth will be like an icy sea, frozen solid. Make the necessary changes. Allow the Holy Spirit to take the lead in your life.

## Third Principle of Change

Determine to be more Christ-like every day.

The quality of the transformation in a moral man is determined by whether he is becoming measurably more like Christ. Let us look at yet another translation of Romans 12:1-2, the New Living Translation.

> *(Romans 12:1-2 NLT) "And so, dear Christian friends, I plead with you to give your bodies to God. Let them be a living and holy sacrifice--the kind he will accept. When you think of what he has done for you, is this too much to ask? {2} Don't copy the behavior and customs of this world, but let God transform you into a new person by changing the way you think. Then you will know what God wants you to do, and you will know how good and pleasing and perfect his will really is."*

Paul's words are not a suggestion. Transformation is a biblical command for biblically-based change. Unless you embrace transformation, it will not occur. The alternative to becoming progressively more like Christ is to be progressively more worldly. There are no other choices. Men who try to sit on the fence between these two worlds will find that, in the end, they conformed to the world. They changed to be more like it, despite their attempts to be content with a static life.

Ultimately, the Lord will measure your eternal significance by the transformation within your life and the lives of the people you touch. There will come a day when you reflect back on your life and do the same. Will the lives of others shine with Christ's light because you came across their paths? Will they give evidence that you have been salt and light to them? If so, Christ will be glorified and you will be satisfied.

Make the decision to welcome change. Renew your mind; contain your thoughts; let the Holy Spirit lead you in every situation; and determine to be more Christ-like. Never accept the inevitability of going through life, being content to remain as you are. Understand your need to learn and grow. Personal transformation is always a decision you make for yourself. Just do it! Get hooked on change.

## An Attitude of Patient and Confident Expectation

You will not always have control over life's circumstances. However, you will have control over your attitudes, whether in the worst or the best of times. An attitude of patience expectation for God's best becomes the incubator for personal transformation.

As a moral man, you can live in the confident expectation that God is at work in your life. Your future is in His hands, and His plan for you is working for your benefit. You will be able to enjoy God's help in controlling your mind, will and emotions. This Spirit-led control gives you the ability to make correct judgments along the way. Then, you will find you are able to control your attitudes with this in mind: There are no surprises in heaven, and God is fully capable of performing His Word over you.

The seasons of change and their timing in your life may not be your choice. You may have to endure particular seasons that seem endless. Nevertheless, you will always have control over one significant factor. You can exercise a patient, faith-filled attitude.

*(Luke 21:19 NKJV) "By your patience possess your souls."*

Change is constant for every man. Only God never changes. If you attempt to secure yourself by trying not to change, it will not work. It is fallacy and pure denial to think you will remain as you are. Do not try to set yourself in a comfort zone. You will be digging a hole in which you will bury your future success and significance. Comfort zones are graves waiting to be filled by men who slide away from their dependence on God. The result is that they deny themselves the opportunity to be transformed and grow through their trust in the Lord. As I have said, transformation, either positive or negative, is inevitable. The ultimate question is, who will control the changes in your life and what will be the results of those changes?

*(Proverbs 3:5-6 NKJV) "Trust in the LORD with all your heart, And lean not on your own understanding; {6} In all your ways acknowledge Him, And He shall direct your paths."*

---

**LIFELINE**
Surrender to change. It will
be liberating, empowering
and will release your
destiny to you.

---

# Part II
# FAITH WILL FLOAT YOUR BOAT.

# Chapter 7

## Fixed on the Light, not the Sting

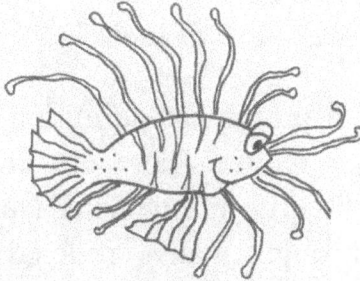

Lionfish

Part I dealt with the moral character of a man who finds safety from sin in God's "shark cage." You read that this cage is composed of the things that keep a man from his own pride or dependence upon self. Every man must realize that God's presence and provision protects him from other dangers too.

Consider the sting of the lionfish. The lionfish is not menacing-looking like a shark. It is beautifully colored, elegant, and graceful in appearance. It tempts you to reach out and touch it. However, if you give in to the temptation, you will be stung by its dangerous, poisonous spines. You will not soon forget the experience. A lionfish will sting anything that gets close to it.

In Part II, you will see how a moral man is to navigate through all the tempting "lionfish of life" without being stung. He does this by faith.

*(Hebrews 11:1 NKJV) "Now faith is the substance of things hoped for, the evidence of things not seen."*

Hebrews 11:1 is a prominent definition of faith most Christians readily recite. There are countless other definitions. My favorite is my wife, Nancy's. It has sustained me through many troubled waters, and reflects the experiences of so many others who continued safely toward their destinies. Here it is.

*Faith is looking into the light and holding onto what you see in the spirit, until it comes to pass.*

---

### LIFELINE
Trust your journey to the excellence of your faith. Trust the outcomes to the excellence of God.

---

# Daniel

Now, let's go swimming with Samswim's friend, Daniel. He has safely navigated the waters of life without tasting the sting of the lionfish (or the bite of the lion). This deadly sting comes in many forms, such as laziness, compromise, self-dependence, or perhaps a number of other temptations. Among these, is the sin with which the devil tried to tempt Daniel, the sin of denying his commitment to God (defilement at its worst). Like touching the beautiful lionfish, contact with compromise of commitment to God can be lethal.

Living as a moral man requires you to embrace an uncompromising position regarding your priorities. God is always to be first. Pleasing Him must be the measure of every circumstance you face. Daniel always honored God, regardless of what he faced. Let's take our example from him. When Daniel was carried away captive to Babylon, he made a choice that became the foundation of his incredibly excellent life. He steadfastly determined in his heart that he would not defile himself.

*(Daniel 1:8 NKJV) "But Daniel purposed in his heart that he would not defile himself with the portion of the king's delicacies, nor with the wine which he drank; therefore he*

*requested of the chief of the eunuchs that he might not defile himself."*

Daniel's decision not to defile himself came from within. It was a choice made with purpose and it defined his character. It was part of him. He never abandoned it. It never abandoned him. He refused to allow his circumstances to determine his attitudes and actions. He was a moral man who did his best in every situation. Daniel kept his heart pure. He focused on God, and was determined to please Him, regardless of what it might cost. His formula for excellence was simple. He trusted God. He always honored Him. He fully depended on him. These were his choices, even when it looked like his circumstances were about to devour him. Then, he behaved according to what he believed. He worshiped as he trusted God, even when the outcome seemed unwelcome, or worse.

*(Daniel 1:8a NKJV) "But Daniel purposed in his heart that he would not defile himself..."*

Daniel was protected through all the dangers he faced because he made a decision not to pollute himself with things that did not please God. Instead, he kept his heart fixed on God. When you face temptations that would compromise your character, keep your heart fixed on the Lord. Refuse to be enticed. Do not touch or be tempted by sin. Maintain an awareness of the presence of God.

## The Sting of Temptation
### (Meet Fred Finfool.)

It is time to meet another of Samswim's friends. He is quite different from Daniel. His name is Fred Finfool. He was swimming in the same waters as Daniel. He had the same opportunities as Daniel. He faced the same predators Daniel and every man faces. Unlike Daniel, he chose to touch what would sting him. He opted for compromise and sin. He failed to remain committed the Lord. He paid the price. It was deadly... and it hurt!

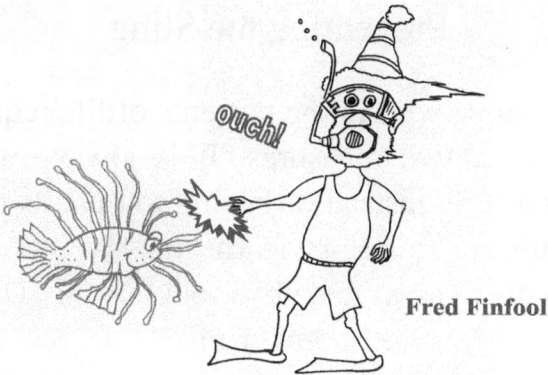

Fred Finfool

## Patterns

The primary difference between Daniel and Fred Finfool was found in what they permitted to dwell in their hearts. What dwells in a man's heart will define the quality of his spirit. Daniel's spirit was excellent, fully pleasing to God. Mr. Finfool's problem was revealed in the patterns of his life. He continually found himself being stung, because he reached out to every attractive-looking enticement that came his way. He lacked Daniel's understanding and wisdom. Like Daniel, Fred Finfool had his opportunities, but chose to be carried away by very different currents of life. He turned from the Spirit of God and allowed himself to live a defiled lifestyle. In time, he found it hurt, but he became so comfortable in his discomfort, that he expected nothing better than sting after sting. He got what he expected.

## Preventing the Sting

A successful swim in the currents of life requires a few preventative measures. It is always wise to prevent a sting instead of having to treat its painful aftermath. You can learn a few of these preventative measures by looking at Daniel's choices. He was a moral man of consistency. He was always a champ, never a chump. He fed his excellent spirit with uncompromising, God-pleasing principles. Consequently, he avoided life's lionfish. He never became the victim in the temptation-infested waters of life.

## The Excellent Spirit in a Moral Man

Daniel, Chapter 5 gives great insight into the characteristics of someone whose manhood reflects the heart of God. It records the blasphemous feast King Belshazzar gave for a thousand of his lords. The feast was an unholy affront to God. The divine, righteous response came as the finger of God wrote on the wall of the king's palace. Belshazzar and his court were terrified at the sight of this. The king called for Daniel because it was widely known that Daniel would be able to interpret the writings. Let the words of this king, spoken to Daniel so many years ago, speak to your heart.

> *(Daniel 5:14 NKJV) "I have heard of you, that the Spirit of God is in you, and that light and understanding and excellent wisdom are found in you."*

Belshazzar's words teach us five championship characteristics found in a moral man with an excellent spirit.

1. The Spirit of God is the abiding and assuring power behind the life and influence of a man of excellence.
2. There is a light shining from men like Daniel. It shines so others can be influenced by who they are and how God is working in them.

*(Matthew 5:14-16 NKJV) "You are the light of the world. A city that is set on a hill cannot be hidden. {15} Nor do they light a lamp and put it under a basket, but on a lampstand, and it gives light to all who are in the house. {16} Let your light so shine before men, that they may see your good works and glorify your Father in heaven."*

3. Daniel had an understanding of how to avoid the sting of temptation. He knew falling into temptation would lead to the throbbing pain of failure. A moral man with an excellent spirit keeps his life pleasing to God, undefiled and pure. Though he cannot be sinless, the motivation of his heart can be consistently to honor God in all things. As he does, he finds that the Lord will honor his heart, and will keep him in all of his ways.

*(Psalms 91:14-16 NKJV) "Because he has set his love upon Me, therefore I will deliver him; I will set him on high, because he has known My name. {15} He shall call upon Me, and I will answer him; I will be with him in trouble; I will deliver him and honor him. {16} With long life I will satisfy him, And show him My salvation."*

4. Men like Daniel strive to gain and retain God's kind of wisdom. This wisdom is a life-giving and life-keeping resource. It enables a man to overcome difficulties, dilemmas and doubts.
5. In times of uncertainty, others will call upon men with excellent spirits.

Your path to success and significance will be safely illuminated by the excellence of your spirit. Be like Daniel. Invite the Spirit of God to have that special place in your heart and surrender the path of your life to the light only He can provide. Then let it shine through you, so that men will see your good works and give God glory!

## Daniel's Choices

As you have seen, Daniel chose to establish a life-style of no compromise. He would not entangle himself with anything that displeased God. In Daniel, Chapter 5, Daniel was called to the palace to interpret the writing on the wall.

*(Daniel 5:16-17 NKJV) "And I have heard of you, that you can give interpretations and explain enigmas. Now if you can read the writing and make known to me its interpretation, you shall be clothed with purple and have a chain of gold around your neck, and shall be the third ruler in the kingdom." {17} Then Daniel answered, and said before the king, "Let your gifts be for yourself, and give your rewards to another; yet I will read the writing to the king, and make known to him the interpretation."*

When Daniel came to the palace, the king tried to buy his ability to explain the unexplainable. Daniel refused the king's offer of riches. He was unwilling to be soiled or defiled by unrighteous greed. His interpretation of the writing would be an act of obedience to God. It would be spoken in prophetic knowledge and wisdom. He was a moral man with an excellent spirit, walking in the gifts of God.

Though he was not afraid to speak the truth to the king, Daniel knew the risk. He understood that the king might react in anger and harm him. Nevertheless, Daniel would not appease the king or lie to him for the sake of his own safety, convenience or gain. He spoke boldly to the king.

*(Daniel 5:22-23 NKJV) "But you his son, Belshazzar, have not humbled your heart, although you knew all this. {23} And you have lifted yourself up against the Lord of heaven... and the God who holds your breath in His hand and owns all your ways, you have not glorified."*

## Excellent Habits

Daniel, Chapter 6 records the plot of Daniel's enemies to entrap him. Would fear tempt Daniel to deny his regular time of communion with God?

*(Daniel 6:7-8 NKJV) "All the governors of the kingdom, the administrators and satraps, the counselors and advisors, have consulted together to establish a royal statute and to make a firm decree, that whoever petitions any god or man for thirty days, except you, O king, shall be cast into the den of lions. {8} Now, O king, establish the decree and sign the writing, so that it cannot be changed, according to the law of the Medes and Persians..."*

The decree that only the king was to be worshiped had been signed. Now Daniel knew the trap was laid. Would he bend to the pressure and change his habits regarding his God?

*(Daniel 6:10 NKJV) "Now when Daniel knew that the writing was signed, he went home. And in his upper room, with his windows open toward Jerusalem, he knelt down on his knees three times that day, and prayed and gave thanks before his God, as was his custom since early days."*

A moral man with an excellent spirit will not bend to pressure. He only bends to God. With a heart filled with trust, he continues to do the right thing. When the trap was laid, Daniel threw open the windows of his home, as was his custom, and prayed to God. He knew that it might cost him his life, but he would not turn from God.

LIFELINE
A moral man of excellent spirit
bends to the will of God alone.

I encourage you to commit to two things. First, define your life by the term *excellence*, as the Scriptures define it. Second, only speak of yourself in ways that affirm you are a winner and champion for Jesus. If you will do these things, you will be well on your way to letting every aspect of your life bring glory to God. When God is glorified, the devil, the lionfish, the sharks and whatever else might swim your way will have to sink into the depths of failure. At the same time, you will rise to the top in success and significance. In this process, others will also see and affirm you as God's winner and champion. Go ahead and live like one. Put your foot on the devil and give him a serious backache!

# Chapter 8

## Avoiding the Fish Fry

### (When you are the Main Course)

## Bend, Bow or Burn?

Now it is time for you to meet Daniel's three friends, Shadrach, Meshach and Abed-Nego. They had been taken captive with Daniel, and brought from Jerusalem to Babylon. They were among the young men chosen to be trained in the palace as future leaders. We do not know much about their personal experiences, but they were as principled and committed to God, as Daniel was. This became evident when King Nebuchadnezzar demanded all those under his rule must gather to bow down and worship a huge golden image he had erected. If they refused, they would be thrown into the fiery furnace. When the time came, as everyone bowed to the image, Daniel's three friends stood upright in their faith, refusing to worship the idol. They knew their devotion to God was revealed for everyone to see. There would be no doubt as to the consequences. Nevertheless, they stood. They would not bow. They would not bend to the pressure. Things were about to heat up.

> *(Daniel 3:21 NKJV) "Then these men were bound in their coats, their trousers, their turbans, and their other garments, and were cast into the midst of the burning fiery furnace."*

Daniel's friends knew that their faithfulness to God would bring them a trip to the furnace. How did they react?

- They did not relent and worship the idol.
- They did not prepare to battle the fire in some desperate hope that they could escape.
- They did not plead for their lives.
- They did not go into the furnace dressed in asbestos suits. They dressed in their trousers and turbans, and all the other garments they wore in their normal pursuit of excellence.
- They did dress in faith.

- They did dress without compromise.
- They did dress for success.

Dress for what you expect beyond the fire. Dress for the supernatural intervention of God. When you are faithful, you can expect your miracle.

---

**LIFELINE**

Men of excellence do not dress for the furnace. They dress for success.

---

*(Daniel 3:22-27 NKJV) "Therefore, because the king's command was urgent, and the furnace exceedingly hot, the flame of the fire killed those men who took up Shadrach, Meshach, and Abed-Nego. {23} And these three men, Shadrach, Meshach, and Abed-Nego, fell down bound into the midst of the burning fiery furnace. {24} Then King Nebuchadnezzar was astonished; and he rose in haste and spoke, saying to his counselors, "Did we not cast three men bound into the midst of the fire?" They answered and said to the king, "True, O king." {25} "Look!" he answered, "I see four men loose, walking in the midst of the fire; and they are not hurt, and the form of*

*the fourth is like the Son of God." {26} Then Nebuchadnezzar went near the mouth of the burning fiery furnace and spoke, saying, "Shadrach, Meshach, and Abed-Nego, servants of the Most High God, come out, and come here." Then Shadrach, Meshach, and Abed-Nego came from the midst of the fire. {27} And the satraps, administrators, governors, and the king's counselors gathered together, and they saw these men on whose bodies the fire had no power; the hair of their head was not singed nor were their garments affected, and the smell of fire was not on them."*

A fourth Man walked into their faithfulness and in that furnace, they became fireproof. They did not bend. They did not bow and *they did not burn!* Daniel's three friends experienced the supernatural intervention of God. Moral men who stay consistent in who and what they are will have the same experience. God will intervene. When you are faith-filled and uncompromising you will be consistently fire-resistant. Shadrach, Meshach and Abed-Nego were not touched by the fire because God faithfully responded to their uncompromising determination to honor and please Him. They were delivered and even promoted. God, who is always faithful, proved to be exactly who He said He was.

```
┌─────────────────────────────┐
│          LIFELINE           │
│   Walk with Jesus. You will │
│       stand the heat.       │
└─────────────────────────────┘
```

# Leading by Example

Countless books have been written on the many ways for men of God to be effective leaders. Among the most highly regarded, are those that teach us to lead by our uncompromising, faith-filled examples. Daniel's three friends were such men. Their example teaches us that our trust in the Lord is rewarded with His divine intervention. Their model of leadership cannot be ignored. They were open books, living epistles of moral manhood. They influenced all who watched, including the king himself. His reaction was to give glory to God. The faith and commitment of Shadrach, Meshach and Abed-Nego confirmed a simple and extremely powerful truth. Let this truth touch your heart as it has mine. Refuse to compromise your devotion to God. Regardless of the cost, it will produce an enormous influence in those around you... and God will come through for you.

Daniel's three friends provide us with a great illustration of God's willingness to respond to the faithfulness and commitment of His servants. Faithfulness and commitment are two primary characteristics of men with excellent spirits. God will give you the same excellence of spirit, if you will embrace the principles that were revealed in the lives of Daniel's friends.

A moral man with an excellent spirit can be sure he will rise to the top. He will have the opportunity to move past the depths and darkness of carnal living to higher, brighter places of shining achievement and honor.

*(Proverbs 20:27 NKJV) "The spirit of a man is the lamp of the LORD, Searching all the inner depths of his heart."*

## The Value of Faithfulness

We saw in Chapter 7, that despite the threat of being thrown into the lion's den, Daniel was faithful to God. He continued to pray. The king had no choice but to honor his decree.

*(Daniel 6:16, 18-22 NKJV) "So the king gave the command, and they brought Daniel*

112

*and cast him into the den of lions. But the king spoke, saying to Daniel, "Your God, whom you serve continually, He will deliver you." ...{18} Now the king went to his palace and spent the night fasting; and no musicians were brought before him. Also his sleep went from him. {19} Then the king arose very early in the morning and went in haste to the den of lions. {20} And when he came to the den, he cried out with a lamenting voice to Daniel. The king spoke, saying to Daniel, "Daniel, servant of the living God, has your God, whom you serve continually, been able to deliver you from the lions?" {21} Then Daniel said to the king, "O king, live forever! {22} My God sent His angel and shut the lions' mouths, so that they have not hurt me, because I was found innocent before Him; and also, O king, I have done no wrong before you.""*

Following Daniel's night in the lion's den, King Darius witnessed firsthand that something supernatural happened because of Daniel's faithfulness to God. It could not be denied that God caged the hunger of those vicious lions, allowing Daniel to spend his night in peace. We can only imagine Daniel's emotions as he experienced the faithful intervention of God in his darkest hour. This miracle made such an impression on the king that he could not help but decree to all the nations under his domain that God was worthy of their respect, honor and fear. King Darius' words clearly illustrate the value of faithfulness.

> *(Daniel 6:25-27 NKJV) "Then King Darius wrote: To all peoples, nations, and languages that dwell in all the earth: Peace be multiplied to you. {26} I make a decree that in every dominion of my kingdom men must tremble and fear before the God of Daniel. For He is the living God, And steadfast forever; His kingdom is the one which shall not be destroyed, And His dominion shall endure to the end. {27} He delivers and rescues, And He works signs and wonders In heaven and on earth, Who has delivered Daniel from the power of the lions."*

Circumstances might have said otherwise, but when Daniel was thrown among the jaws of the predators, there were no bites. I can imagine Daniel using the lions' furry manes for pillows, and sleeping in the assurance that his God would preserve him. He walked out of the lion's den as a living testimony to God's faithfulness. The issue for Daniel was never about what he was going through. It was about the One who was going through it with him.

```
LIFELINE
A moral man's only issue is not
what he is going through. His only
issue is to be faithful to the One
who is going through it with him.
```

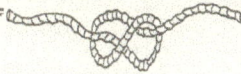

*(Psalms 59:17 NKJV) "To You, O my Strength, I will sing praises; For God is my defense, My God of mercy."*

God is forever faithful, able... and always willing. Be faithful to God.

## The Power of Commitment

Daniel found his commitment to God honored by God's commitment to him. Yes, God did more than preserve Daniel's life. He showered him with great favor. This divine favor followed Daniel right into the lions' den. God heaped mountains of protection and then abundant blessings upon the foundation of Daniel's commitment to Him. God will do the same for you.

*(Daniel 6:28 NKJV)"So this Daniel prospered in the reign of Darius and in the reign of Cyrus the Persian."*

---

### LIFELINE
There are no surprises in heaven, but there are multitudes of wonderful surprises from heaven.

---

What you are about to read has the potential to change your life. Take the time to consider each of the following ten qualities of a committed, faithful moral man. They are gleaned from Daniel's example. Use them to take inventory within your heart. Consider them as guidance in learning how to make your life a journey of faithfulness. Each is obtainable. Take this opportunity to make the necessary changes. Your life will give testimony to the redeeming and enabling power of God.

## A Committed and Faithful Man

1. ...chooses holiness in every situation. He purposes in his heart that he will not do anything to displease God, regardless of what it might cost.
2. ...does not need to promote himself. God will

respond to his commitment and do the promoting in ways no man could.

3. ...will consistently display godly character as the visibly defining mark of his life.

4. ...builds his character on his determination to pray. Consistency of prayer is his badge of excellence. He refuses to be denied his opportunity to commune with God.

5. ...has a thankful spirit. He remains thankful, even when the outcome does not seem good. His thankfulness strengthens his faithfulness. It never wavers, and never fails.

6. ...regards no demand from anyone above his demands on himself to stay fully committed to God.

7. ...never allows the cost of his commitment to be the deciding factor. Honoring and pleasing God are always the deciding factors.

8. ...will survive his trials and walk out of them with dignity and victory.

9. ...sees himself as a champion for Jesus.

10. ...is a winner even when his natural circumstances call him a loser. He wins because he maintains all nine of the previous qualities. He wins because God has eternal rewards that will far outweigh the natural circumstances. Ultimately, he wins because God calls him a winner.

You may have to swim with the lionfish of life and maneuver around the sting of their tentacles. You may have to swim with sharks and seek the refuge of God's protection. In all these things, you can be assured that by being excellent in spirit and faithfully committed to God, you will surface a winner and champion. You will say, *"All is well."*

### Romans 8:38-39: My Paraphrase

*"Moral man of God, I am persuaded that neither death nor life, nor angels nor principalities nor powers, nor things present nor things to come, {39} nor height nor depth, nor any other created thing, including* **lionfish stings, shark bites, persecutions, jealousies, disappointments, dangers or any of life's circumstances (not even lions' dens)** *shall be able to separate you from the love of God which is in Christ Jesus our Lord."*

Let my paraphrase of the Apostle Paul's great words ingrain these thoughts in your heart.

- ☑ You are not a wimp.
- ☑ You are not a chump.
- ☑ You are God's champ!
- ☑ You are a moral man.
- ☑ You have an excellent spirit.
- ☑ You are more than a conqueror and destined for glory!

# Chapter 9

## Walking above the Bite of a Man's Emotions

Meet Willy the Wet Water Walker.

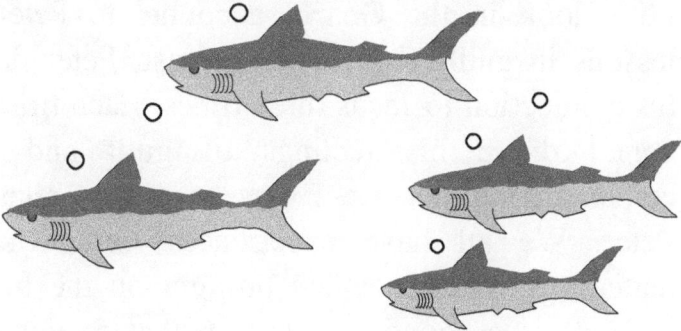

It is time to meet another of Samswim's friends, Willie the Wet Water Walker. He is an interesting fellow. He was previously a man who was deeply troubled. Then, he met Jesus. Now, he can testify to the power of God. His relationship with the Lord and his trust in His Word enabled Willie to overcome four particular emotional dangers found in every man's ocean. These are (1) guilt, (2) shame, (3) sorrow and (4) bitterness.

There has been only one perfect Man, the Lord Jesus Christ. The rest of us are imperfect, fallen human beings. We have all made waves that have damaged others, because they found themselves in the wake of our paths. To deny this is to deny our fallen human nature, and invite it to take a bite out of us. In this chapter, we will examine the effects, and remedies for these four particular emotional dangers: guilt, shame, sorrow and bitterness.

## Drowning in Guilt

Let's look in the Gospel accounts to Peter for lessons in guilt. Upon Jesus' arrest, Peter denied his connection to Jesus three times. Each time, his denial drove his feelings of guilt and self-condemnation deeper. Every man can relate to Peter. We all have experienced certain sinful patterns of failure, which brought on the bite of guilt. It is a foundational truth that to deny the reality of our human frailty is to deny Scripture.

*(Romans 3:23 NKJV) "for all have sinned and fall short of the glory of God,"*

What grieved Peter and caused him so much pain was his guilt for not standing with Christ. He denied his Lord and in doing so surrendered his moral manhood. When a man denies what he knows is right and true, he forfeits the opportunity to live free. He surrenders to the weight of sin. He carries it and staggers under its heavy burden. His guilt overpowers him as it grasps him in its jaws and drags him down, with that sinking feeling... all the way to the bottom. We all face our battles with guilt. Many good men have drowned in it.

Of course, Jesus knew Peter failed. He was fully aware of Peter's abandonment of him. He had even told Peter that it would happen. (As a previous LIFELINE stated, there are no surprises in heaven.) Peter was broken by his failure. He found himself slowly twisting in the jaws of his guilt. When Jesus appeared, glorified in the power of His resurrection, His words to Peter were revealing. Three times, Jesus asked Peter a simple question, *"Do you love Me?"* He did not repeat this question because He missed Peter's first two answers. He did this so that Peter could understand the importance for a moral man to love God. Here was Peter's Lord and Savior, standing before him in His resurrected body. He loved Peter so much that he willingly went to the cross for him (and for us). Jesus did three eternally powerful things. First, He forgave Peter. Second, He challenged Peter to consider how real his love for Jesus was. Third, He gave Peter a task with a purpose that would remove the guilt. He did it through repetition.

*(John 21:15b NKJV) "...Feed My lambs."*
*(John 21:16b NKJV) "...Tend My sheep."*
*(John 21:17b NKJV) "Feed My sheep."*

Then, Jesus gave Peter another command. It was this one upon which Peter would build a life free from guilt. Obedience to this command was to be the door to Peter's freedom. If you are struggling with voices from the past that accuse you, label you and try to convince you defeat is your portion, let this command to Peter be the same for you. Here it is.

*(John 21:19b NKJV) "...And when He had spoken this, He said to him, "Follow Me.""*

When you determine you will follow Jesus, guilt has no right to remain in your heart. You will swim in a sea of forgiveness and blessings. Embrace this truth as you say goodbye to guilt.

*(Romans 8:24 NKJV) "being justified freely by His grace through the redemption that is in Christ Jesus,"*

To be justified means you have been declared not guilty in God's eyes. As a committed, obedient follower of Christ, you are now free of guilt and condemnation. If you still struggle with guilt, then you are allowing a lie to take you under. It has no right to do so. Start walking above the bite of your emotions. Say goodbye to guilt. Walk on the water!

## Sinking in Shame

Shame is not guilt. Guilt is knowing you have made a mistake and sinned, causing God or some other person to be grieved or hurt. Shame is even worse. It is thinking *you are the mistake*. Shame may be defined as feelings of humiliation, dishonor, and worthlessness. It is a loss of self-worth and self-respect. This causes feelings of self-contempt and disgrace that will not leave. For a believer, it is snare from the pit of hell. Feelings of shame may be brought on by the actions of others, or in many cases, by what were a man's own foolish, destructive actions. If shame finds a home in a man's heart, it will be deadly, eating away at him like a cancer.

# Three Oceans of Shame

Samswim's friend, Willie the Wet Water Walker has not only overcome guilt, but he has seen the power of God lift him from under oceans of shame. His eyes are fixed on his destiny. His heart is clear. His steps are ordered by the Lord. Each step is solid and sure. To understand how this happened to Willie, and how it can happen to you, we need to look into the three ways shame pollutes the waters of a man's life.

## 1. Shame because of something done
### *to you by someone else*

Shark bites or lionfish stings usually happen because the swimmer is unaware of the danger. This first category of shame usually occurs in a man's youth (though it can happen later in life). It comes when, as a child, a man was the victim of some degrading act of physical, verbal or sexual abuse. These kinds of humiliating, violent, evil acts leave a man victim to memories and emotions that say he was dirty and used. He sees himself as an object of shame, contempt and disgrace. In some way, he feels responsible for the shame.

A man could also be drowning in shame because, unknown to him, someone drew his wife into committing adultery or homosexuality. When he discovered her transgressions, and especially if they became public knowledge, it was devastating and humiliating. It generated shame-filled feelings of inadequacy and embarrassment.

Other men may have been lied to and enticed into a business deal, not knowing it was dishonest, and were subsequently caught up in its discovery. They were publicly prosecuted and perhaps even jailed for it. Now the shame of this public humiliation lives with them constantly.

There are many other reasons men live with feelings of shame that someone else put upon them. In every one of these cases, the shame is a feeling and a lie. When a man is a born-again Christian, he is positioned to overcome this lie. When the devil tries to accuse you and tempt you into believing that you deserve the shame because of what someone else did, speak the Word to him. *Devil, this is written about me...*

*(Joel 2:26-27 NKJV) "'You shall eat in plenty and be satisfied, And praise the name of the LORD your God, Who has dealt wondrously with you; And My people shall never be put to shame. Then you shall know that I am in the midst of Israel: I am the LORD your God And there is no other. My people shall never be put to shame.'"*

*(Romans 8:1 NKJV) "There is therefore now no condemnation to those who are in Christ Jesus, who do not walk according to the flesh, but according to the Spirit."*

After you have said these things to the devil, start saying them to yourself. Then, begin to live what you say. You will be speaking the truth and it will set you free.

## 2. Shame because of something *you did to someone else*

Let us look at an example of such a man. We read about him in Genesis, Chapter 38. His name was Judah. When his son died, Judah told his son's widow, Tamar, to live without a husband until his other son, Shelah was old enough for him to marry her. However, when Shelah had grown up, Judah did not arrange for the marriage, as he had promised. This caused Tamar to be bitter, because she had remained without a husband for so many years.

Tamar decided to get revenge. She dressed herself as a prostitute, covered her face and waited on the road until Judah walked by. When he approached her, he did not recognize her, and she enticed him into her bed. They agreed that she would receive a young goat as payment, which he would later send her. She demanded his signet ring, cord and shepherd's staff as security until he could send her the goat. He agreed and gave them to her. Here is what followed.

> *(Genesis 38:20-26 NKJV) "And Judah sent the young goat by the hand of his friend the Adullamite, to receive his pledge from the woman's hand, but he did not find her. {21} Then he asked the men of that place, saying, "Where is the harlot who was openly by the roadside?" And they said, "There was no harlot in this place." {22} So he returned to Judah and said, "I cannot find her. Also, the men of the place said there was no harlot in this place." {23} Then Judah said, "Let her take them for herself, **lest we be shamed**; for I sent this young goat and you have not found her." {24} And it came to pass, about three months after, that Judah was told, saying, "Tamar your daughter-in-law has*

*played the harlot; furthermore she is with child by harlotry." So Judah said, "Bring her out and let her be burned!" {25} When she was brought out, she sent to her father-in-law, saying, "By the man to whom these belong, I am with child." And she said, "Please determine whose these are; the signet and cord, and staff." {26} So Judah acknowledged them and said, **"She has been more righteous than I, because I did not give her to Shelah my son."** And he never knew her again."*

Judah's sin found him out. He and Tamar used each other in a way contrary to God's Word. Perhaps you have done the same. Have you taken advantage of someone (not just sexually)? Were your actions shameful and dishonorable? Have you accepted shame as a fitting garment, a garment of heaviness, a straight jacket of unworthiness? Your shameful act is not the unforgivable sin. It does, however, invite a real and very evil spirit to become your traveling companion. It can get under your skin and fester. It can bring a flood of painful emotions. Like Judah, you must acknowledge your sin and repent. Then, accept God's forgiveness, in Jesus' name. It will drive out the shame.

Here is a final thought on this kind of shame. You may never completely get past the regrets. That is sometimes just the way it is. The key is to look ahead and commit to honoring God with how you live the rest of your life. Doing so will position you for great things. Turn your devastating circumstance into someone else's blessing and it will become yours too.

*(2 Corinthians 5:17 NKJV) "Therefore, if anyone is in Christ, he is a new creation; old things have passed away; behold, all things have become new."*

## 3. Shame because of something
### *you did to yourself*

In Luke, chapter 15, we read about a young man who demanded his inheritance from his father and then went away to waste it all on a sinful, self-destructive lifestyle. He ended up destitute and without hope. He barely survived by feeding another man's pigs. Here is what the Word of God says about the rest of his story.

*(Luke 15: 17-24 NKJV} "But when he came to himself, he said, 'How many of my father's hired servants have bread enough and to spare, and I perish with hunger! {18a, 19} I will arise and go to my father, and will say... **'I am no longer worthy to be called your son.** Make me like one of your*

*hired servants.' {20} And he arose and came to his father. But when he was still a great way off, his father saw him and had compassion, and ran and fell on his neck and kissed him. {21} And the son said to him, 'Father, I have sinned against heaven and in your sight, and am no longer worthy to be called your son.'{22} But the father said to his servants, 'Bring out the best robe and put it on him, and put a ring on his hand and sandals on his feet. {23} And bring the fatted calf here and kill it, and let us eat and be merry; {24} for this my son was dead and is alive again; he was lost and is found.' And they began to be merry."*

These are particularly bitter waters in which to swim. Have you been the cause of your own misfortune? Have poor, prideful or arrogant decisions succeeded in destroying your self-respect and devastating your life? Have you messed up everything? Are you ashamed of yourself? Do as the young man did in Luke 15. Return now to your heavenly Father. Confess your sin to Him. He will celebrate His forgiveness over you and your position will again be an honored one, not a shameful one. Hebrews 11:16 says of those who have faith in God, and who turn from their sins, that, *"God is not ashamed to be called their God."*

Let's be clear about what you must do to change how you feel. By the way, I have not yet met a man who was completely free of shameful feelings. As I said earlier, the only Man who ever lived a perfect life was Jesus. So, do not discount what you have read. Embrace it and apply it to your own heart. You will find it liberating. Just be honest with yourself. Do not expect an instant and complete elimination of the feelings. It will take your determination and consistency to overcome them completely. Here is the process. Be faithful to it and you will destroy any feelings of shame. Say goodbye to shame.

*(2 Corinthians 10:5 NKJV) "casting down arguments and every high thing that exalts itself against the knowledge of God, bringing every thought into captivity to the obedience of Christ."*

## Sorrow

Sorrow is defined as "a state of distress caused by loss, disappointment, grief, sadness or regret."[4] Here is the first thing any man should understand if he has been sinking under the weight of sorrow. Like guilt and shame, sorrow is a feeling. It was imposed and now is maintained by a combination of two things. First, there are memories a man revisits that maintain his feelings of sorrow. Second, he assumes it is inevitable that there will be no improvement in the future. Together, his feelings and assumptions dominate him and keep him captive to his sorrows.

If you are living with sorrow, it is a fact that what brought on the sorrow was real. That cannot be changed. What you can change are your assumptions and expectations for the future. Therefore, the key to breaking out of the sorrow is to focus on changing how you think about your future. We looked at this in Chapter 6. Now let's go a little deeper.

> *(Romans 12:2 NLT) "Don't copy the behavior and customs of this world, but let God transform you into a new person by*

---

[4] Dictionary.com, Unabridged, Based on the Random House Unabridged Dictionary © Random House, Inc. 2010 - an iPhone application.

*changing the way you think. Then you will know what God wants you to do, and you will know how good and pleasing and perfect his will really is."*

In Romans 12:2, Paul wrote about a man's ability to change, by allowing himself to think differently about his past experiences and their effects on his present view of himself. Paul certainly knew the captivating power of sorrow-filled memories. He had more than his share of them. They could have held him down, but he refused to allow this. Like every man, Paul had to find a way to get past his memories and take himself to a productive, peaceful place where he could reach his potential. He had to find a way to become a God-pleasing moral man... and he did.

Romans 12:2 reveals a five-step process for overcoming sorrow. A man who follows Christ can claim this process for his own.

1. Do not continue to think as you have in the past. Your world has changed.
2. Invite God to have dominion over your thinking. This will allow Him to transform you into a new man.
3. Begin to look ahead and allow the significance of the past, with its hold on your emotions, to fade. You will discover and claim new God-

given assumptions concerning your potential, and expectations for your future.

4. Embrace a new set of biblical facts, based on the understanding you have gained. Then let them be the measure of your feelings.

5. No longer give sorrow an invitation to speak into your life. Silence its voice by keeping these words from the Prophet Isaiah close to your heart. They are more than a suggestion. They are a combination of God's command and promise for you. Say goodbye to sorrow.

*(Isaiah 43:18-19 NKJV) "Do not remember the former things, Nor consider the things of old. {19} Behold, I will do a new thing, Now it shall spring forth; Shall you not know it? I will even make a road in the wilderness And rivers in the desert."*

## Bitten with Bitterness

Of these four dangerous emotions that want to inhabit every man's ocean, bitterness has perhaps the nastiest bite. It can be the most punishing and constraining. Bitterness grows from seeds of unforgiveness. If you are living with bitterness, it is likely that you have played the blame game. By this, I mean you have blamed someone (rightly or wrongly) for the situation in which you find yourself. Perhaps you blamed God. Maybe you even blamed yourself, or just life. Many of us have combined some or all of these and given them a home in our hearts. The bitterness began as unforgiveness and blame, but grew into something far more dangerous. This is a fair description of how many men find themselves in the cruel bondage of hardened, bitter hearts.

If you are living in bitterness, you have just read how the process captured you. Let's be accurate in understanding this process. What happened may or may not have been your choice. It began when you surrendered to unforgiveness and played the blame game. This was solely your choice and in time, you soured to the point of bitterness. It went deeply into your soul and gripped your emotions. Then, it captured your attitudes and held your future in its jaws. What can be done? Turn to the remedy Scripture provides. Peter's question to the Lord is the classic Scriptural example of how to shed the shackles of unforgiveness and blame, with their offspring, bitterness.

> *(Matthew 18:21-35 NKJV) "Then Peter came to Him and said, "Lord, how often shall my brother sin against me, and I forgive him? Up to seven times?" {22} Jesus said to him, "I do not say to you, up to seven times, but up to seventy times seven.""*

Defeating unforgiveness and blame is often a battle... no, a series of battles. Every man has to fight these battles until the victory comes. If the unforgiveness and blame show up again, fight the battle again. You must drive them back every time they reappear. You must deny them the opportunity to spread their destructive seeds. If bitterness is already alive and well in your heart, kill it with the surefire weapon God has given you. This weapon is a combination of forgiveness and your refusal to play the blame game. Do not be surprised that it will take repeated efforts. As this becomes your habitual, repetitive reaction to the past, it will destroy the bitterness in which you have been trapped.

There is one more thing about which you should be aware. Bitterness is particularly destructive because it feeds on not only unforgiveness and the blame game, but also gains additional strength by pulling on your pride. When you feel like you are swimming in bitterness, and you continually nurture this feeling, you can be sure that your pride is there feeding it. Bitterness grows fat on pride. The solution is to starve it out of existence. Do this with humility and forgiveness.

It is time for a new beginning. You can walk far above the destruction. Make the decision to reject guilt, shame, sorrow and bitterness. It is a new day. Old things have passed away and all things have become new... if you will let them. Say goodbye to bitterness.

*(2 Corinthians 5:17 NKJV) "Therefore, if anyone is in Christ, he is a new creation; old things have passed away; behold, all things have become new."*

---

**LIFELINE**

Look for God's new thing. It is yours.

---

# Chapter 10

# Faith will float Your Boat

A moral man's boat floats on two issues. The first is having the faith to seek God's direction for his life. This determines the set of his sail and thus, points the way to his destiny. Second, he floats his boat on his determination to stay on the course he believes God has set for him. He diligently strives to maintain his heading. He never loses the dream of his destiny. It may yet to be fully defined, but he knows it is out there. He sticks to his course until the day he clearly sees it on the horizon. Then he rejoices and presses on until that final day when his faith is fulfilled and he safely reaches his destination. After that, it is party time! A great celebration supper awaits him, with Jesus at the head of the table, giving His eternal prize to this man who finished.

> *(2 Timothy 4:7-8 NLT) "I have fought a good fight, I have finished the race, and I have remained faithful. {8} And now the prize awaits me..."*

A moral man's journey through his life requires the ability to manage the trip in good weather and bad. He must know how to sail through the storms he inevitably will encounter. There are four things vital to keeping his boat afloat and on course.

1. He must have absolute faith in his Navigator.
2. He must hear the voice of his Navigator.
3. He must understand the directions he gets from his Navigator. (By now, I am sure you understand that his Navigator is the Holy Spirit.)
4. He must have the wisdom to follow the directions given by his Navigator, so he can sail through both sunshine and storm.

Without these vital ingredients, a moral man risks meeting three distinct and particularly dangerous faith-killing fish. I call them "devilfish," because they fit the description of one of the ocean's deepest swimming denizens. On occasion, they may be found lurking just below the surface, waiting for their opportunity to attack your faith. These three devilfish are (1) distractions, (2) disillusionment and (3) dread. They are ready to devour any man who finds himself losing his footing and slipping beneath the stormy waves.

First Devilfish:
## Distractions

Distractions are those things or people that prevent you from maintaining the faith and focus that keep you on course. Distractions want to dump you into an ocean of confusion, and draw you away from your destination.

You can expect to find distractions at any time or place on the journey to your destiny. They will surely await you. You cannot avoid them, but you can prevent them from sending you overboard and into the predatory jaws waiting beneath the waves. How can you overcome the inevitable distractions the storms of life bring to every man? I want to share with you some biblical principles that will keep your feet firmly on deck, as you maintain the faith and focus necessary to avoid shipwreck. Here is how to follow the Navigator's instructions and sail with a fair wind.

1. Be selective in what you allow your mind to dwell upon. Be aware of what you are thinking. Do not allow distractions or negative thoughts any opportunity to influence you unduly. Steer your thinking toward what Paul described in his advice to the Philippian and Colossian believers.

   *(Philippians 4:8 NKJV) "Finally, brethren, whatever things are true, whatever things are noble, whatever things are just, whatever things are pure, whatever things are lovely, whatever things are of good report, if there is any virtue and if there is anything praiseworthy; meditate on these things."*

   *(Colossians 3:1-2 NKJV) "If then you were raised with Christ, seek those things which are above, where Christ is, sitting at the right hand of God. {2} Set your mind on things above, not on things on the earth."*

2. Focus on your course. Pay attention to where you are going. Do not get distracted by doing what does not fit with the set of your sail.

3. Do not be distracted by the need for immediate gratification. In today's world, attention spans have been shortened by the technologies with which we live. Sound bites, internet searches, video clips, advertising and the speed of computers all contribute to the expectation and yes, demand for quick results. As a society, we have lost patience with traditional processes. Technology consumes ever-growing amounts of our time, and comes with assumptions that we will not have to wait. God's plan and the course He lays out for you will require you to operate on His timetable, not the world's or yours. This will bring frustrations, because there will be seasons within your journey through life that bring little or no immediate gratification. Do not allow frustration to become a distraction.

The answer to distraction is to understand you are not alone on your journey. Cling to your faith in the divine Navigator, The Holy Spirit. He is assigned to you. He will never leave you or forsake you. Here is my advice.

- Rejoice in His presence, with great joy.
- Listen to His concerns.

- Believe His promises.
- Follow His directions.
- Allow patience to produce faith. Then, your faith will produce maturity.
- In God's timing, your maturity will take you to your destiny.

*(Proverbs 3:5-6 NKJV) "Trust in the LORD with all your heart, And lean not on your own understanding; {6} In all your ways acknowledge Him, And He shall direct your paths."*

*Proverbs 3:6, My Paraphrase*

*In all your ways acknowledge your divine Navigator and He will set your course.*

## Second Devilfish: Disillusionment

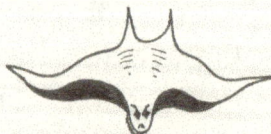

To be disillusioned is to be convinced that your faith, hopes and dreams will never become reality. Disillusionment lies to you about your future and preys on your uncertainty. It works to persuade you to give up. It does this to prevent you from achieving your purposes. The greatest lie of disillusionment is that you would be better off to abandon your course of faith and try something else. The storms you will face carry within them the potential to send you overboard and into the jaws of disillusionment. To stay on course, heed the following principles.

1. Be realistic in your expectations. Take care to align them with the promises you find in what God says in His Word. He will never lie to you.

   *(Numbers 23:19 NKJV) "God is not a man, that He should lie, Nor a son of man, that He should repent. Has He said, and will He not do? Or has He spoken, and will He not make it good?"*

2. Firmly resolve that you will not be driven off course by the setbacks every man experiences. Refuse to be shackled and thrown overboard by disillusionment or unbelief. Continue to trust your Navigator. (By this time you have seen that I am big on trusting God.)

3. Maintain your confession that the Holy Spirit sets your destination and travels to it with you. He will give you the set of your sail and point the way. He will inspire and encourage you, and will surely take you to your destination. You may be a captain on your ship, but the One with you is of the highest authority. Speak the Word to disillusionment when it comes.

   *(Philippians 1:6 NKJV) "being confident of this very thing, that He who has begun a*

*good work in you will complete it until the day of Jesus Christ;"*

```
LIFELINE
Maintain your confession and He
will watch over your course.
```

### Third Devilfish: Dread

The best way to describe dread is to call it an unreasonable, exaggerated fear of some imagined experience or outcome. What you dread was not on your schedule of stops along the way to your destiny. Dread is stronger than fear because it tries to terrorize you into considering the worst of the worst. If you allow it to, it will sink your boat and spill you into deeply troubled waters. Dread replaces your trust in the Lord with a sense of helplessness and resignation. It convinces you to embrace a conviction that the worst that you could imagine will happen. Dread is among the nastiest of the monsters that lurk under the stormy seas of life. It has a hunger to do violence to your heart. It wants to confuse and disrupt your thinking. Allowing dread to have its way will leave you powerless to resist its bite… and it will bite!

*(James 1:2-4 NKJV) "My brethren, count it all joy when you fall into various trials, {3} knowing that the testing of your faith produces patience. {4} But let patience have its perfect work, that you may be perfect and complete, lacking nothing."*

The answer to dread is to speak to it in faith. If dread tries to fill your heart with darkness, and panic begins to set in, do as Jesus did. Exercise the authority of God. Speak to your dread.

*(Mark 4:35-40 NKJV) "On the same day, when evening had come, He said to them, "Let us cross over to the other side." {36} Now when they had left the multitude, they took Him along in the boat as He was. And other little boats were also with Him. {37} And a great windstorm arose, and the waves beat into the boat, so that it was already filling. {38} But He was in the stern, asleep on a pillow. And they awoke Him and said to Him, "Teacher, do You not care that we are perishing?" {39} Then He arose and rebuked the wind, and said to the sea,* **"Peace, be still!" And the wind ceased and there was a great calm.** *{40} But He said to them, "Why are you so fearful?* **How is it that you have no faith?""***

The original Greek word for *"fearful,"* that Mark used in Verse 40, has dread as one of its primary meanings. Let me paraphrase what Jesus said to His disciples.

*Why is it you are so full of dread? How is it that you have not allowed yourself to **speak with faith and cancel your dread?***

When feelings of dread are about to throw you overboard, gather your determination, take a deep breath and destroy them. Speak faith to your feelings, your storm, and your own heart.

*Peace, be still, in Jesus name!*

Only chumps allow themselves to sink into the jaws of distractions, disillusionment and dread. You, moral man of God, are more than able to maintain your course. You are a champ!

## Faith in the Navigator

Faith in your Navigator, the Spirit of God, is the foundation upon which you will float your boat. Your ability to stay out of reach of distraction, disillusionment and dread will depend on keeping your faith fixed on God. This is the deciding factor that determines if you will withstand the storms. You must make the decision to abide in the confident expectation that your Navigator is with you in the boat, and is willing and able to guide you through every storm.

## Abiding in Expectant Faith

To abide means to stay in a particular condition without seeking to change. You make your own choices about where you will abide. Do not choose to abide in storms, circumstances, troubles... and not even those times when everything is all right. God wants you to go beyond the natural, and sail your boat into His supernatural provision and protection. It is fully an act of faith for you to do so. You are to abide in the expectation that God has prepared a journey for you. Abide in faith.

> *(Philippians 3:13-14 NKJV) "Brethren, I do not count myself to have apprehended; but one thing I do, forgetting those things which are behind and reaching forward to those things which are ahead, {14} I press toward the goal for the prize of the upward call of God in Christ Jesus."*

Too many of us try to abide in the present. To succeed, you must disturb the present. Staying in one place, whether in a storm or the calm, is an invitation for a visit from lionfish, sharks, devilfish, and whatever else lurks beneath the waves. We often make ourselves content with whatever comforts or discomforts we have. If you enrolled in an MBA course, they would teach you that most business failures can be attributed directly to people who refuse to move from their comfort zones. Refusing to change because of lack of faith is deadly. God has already provided you with a future and a hope. Without it, today becomes a six-sided box with no tomorrow.

---

**LIFELINE**

To succeed, you must disturb the present.

---

The qualities of the present must not determine whether you ought to move on to the future. It may be good, bad or ugly today... but tomorrow is another day. The present can only give you what you already have, or what already has you. God wants to give you so much more. If you try to be content with the present, you quickly find yourself passed by and missing the blessings. You cannot capture the present. It quickly fades into the past. Determine to abide in faith, expecting the supernatural intervention of God. Expect it. Believe it. Receive it!

Growth is fully a function of the future. Abide in the expectation that God has only just begun a good work in you. As you journey in faith, He will complete it until the day He comes back for you. His plan for you is one you just cannot afford to pass up. It is so rich with His presence that it would be foolish to be content to drop your anchor in the present. Embrace your expectations for the future. Then, the negatives that weigh you down and try to sink you will give way to the positives. God's plan for you is the best. Expect it! Abide in the expectation of fair weather. The storms will have to bow to your faith. If you want to succeed, disturb the present with a healthy dose of determination. You will be the champion God made you to be. Chumps stay in the storm. Champs move ahead with God.

---

LIFELINE
Growth is fully a function of the future.

---

## Your Four Abiding Expectations

Abram is a fine biblical example of a moral man who abided in the expectations of his faith.

*(Genesis 12:1-3 NKJV) "Now the LORD had said to Abram: "Get out of your country, From your family And from your father's house, To a land that I will show you. {2} I will make you a great nation; I will bless you And make your name great; And you shall be a blessing. {3} I will bless those who bless you, And I will curse him who curses you; And in you all the families of the earth shall be blessed.""*

God challenged Abram to leave his present life behind, to dream big dreams and embrace his potential. It would be an act of faith. Nothing else would float Abram's boat. Here is my paraphrase of what God said to Abram.

*Abram, leave everything, all that is familiar, safe and comfortable. Journey to the place I will show you. It is a place I am giving you. I will cause you to progressively **increase**, and your greatness will fill a nation. Your **excellent reputation** will be known to all, and your moral manhood will influence others so they may know of my goodness. I will **intervene supernaturally** in all your affairs to reward those who bless you. Those who try to bring evil upon you will know the wrath of My judgment. As you walk on the waters of your faith, you shall have **a truly***

**significant life**. *From you will spring forth a blessing for all mankind. His name is Christ the Lord.*

## Your First Expectation: Increase

To increase means to become progressively greater in size, amount, number and intensity. To increase is to enlarge, expand and make room for greater capacity. Notice my paraphrase above labels the increase as progressive. The progress we make follows our willingness to move ahead in faith. God said something like this.

*Abram, you have a nice comfortable life here. It is secure being in your father Terah's shadow, but I want to take you to a bigger place that will make you a bigger man. I want your faith to progressively increase and strengthen, until you fulfill your destiny and become known as a giant of faith. This will only happen if you will abide in the expectation of a great journey with Me. Embrace the future and put feet to your faith. Abram, expect the increase!*

Perhaps it is time for you to abide in the expectation for increase in your future. My advice to you is to get up, set your sail and get going.

## Your Second Expectation: Excellence

God encouraged Abram that in the future his excellent reputation would be known to all. He could expect that his influence would bring countless others to know of the Lord's goodness. As others acknowledge your moral standards of excellence, your reputation will grow. Your willingness to abide in the expectation of your own excellence will secure your future. Step out in obedience. Your faith will take you to the promises of God. Your moral character will keep you there. When you expect, and even demand excellence in yourself, you will become all you can be. You will do everything God placed in your heart. You will influence your world as a man of great faith, moral excellence and eternally fruitful accomplishments.

You can float your boat in perfect peace as you make your way through the currents of life. God wants you to be an excellent reflection of Him at work in you. I strongly encourage you to let God mold and shape your life. If you allow Him, He will shape you even more into an unsinkable vessel of honor. You will never need to worry about capsizing and sinking into dangerous waters. Will you expect excellence as your portion, your future and your testimony?

# Your Third Expectation: The Supernatural Intervention of God

The first two expectations I have suggested lead to this third one. When you demand of yourself a consistent increase in your faith and excellence in your pursuit of God, you can have confidence that God is with you. When necessary, you can expect His inevitable supernatural intervention. Our biblical model of this was found in Genesis 12:3. God assured Abram that He would intervene supernaturally in his affairs, blessing whoever blessed Abram and visiting His wrath upon those who tried to bring evil upon him.

Regardless of the walls and barriers you face, or threats and attacks you are confronted with, God will be there. You can abide in the expectation that He will stand between you and the attacker. He will carry you through when you seem to be over your head, floundering in deep waters. He will assure you that He is the great I AM, forever faithful to His Word. I have seen Him intervene countless times in my life. Recalling my experiences with His faithfulness always builds my faith. I have well learned these powerful truths from Psalm 91. Let His voice speak to you through them, as it has to me.

*(Psalms 91:14-16 NKJV) "Because he has set his love upon Me, therefore I will deliver him; I will set him on high, because he has known My name. {15} He shall call upon Me, and I will answer him; I will be with him in trouble; I will deliver him and honor him. {16} With long life I will satisfy him, And show him My salvation."*

My faith strengthens each time I read Verse 15. I know it will do the same for you. Let me share with you my paraphrase of this verse.

*When you call upon Me, I will answer you. I will remove the trouble in which you find yourself, and replace it with my blessings. I will do this because of your uncompromising faith in me. Your choice to unconditionally serve and honor Me has stirred My heart and set it in motion. Now I will demonstrate the evidence of My saving power. I am ready to fulfill and perform My Word over you.*

It would be easy to testify of the times when God rescued me from the illnesses and unforeseen circumstances that could have rattled my cage... but for my faith in His faithfulness. Instead, let me share with you a little different and perhaps a bit humorous account of how Psalm 91:15 worked in my life.

It was in 1997, when I was teaching at New Covenant International Bible School in Auckland, New Zealand. We often had opportunities to do evangelistic preaching and street ministry. On one such occasion, we went to one of the poorest, most crime-ridden neighborhoods in the city. I was the designated preacher that afternoon.

We set up our sound equipment on the steps in front of a market, which was next to a number of stores. These included the neighborhood pool hall. The pool hall was off to the left side of me and at a right angle to the steps we were using. It was impossible not to notice a group of tough-looking young men who were standing in front of the pool hall. Throughout the afternoon, as we went through our program, these young, tough-looking guys continued to hang out, watching us. The crowd was mostly Pacific Islanders. Off to the right side of me was a burley, muscular man in a wheel chair. During the singing and skits we were doing, it became obvious to me that he was demon-possessed. He hooted, growled, and made awful, distracting noises. He looked genuinely dangerous. I had a foreboding feeling in my heart and began earnestly to pray. Finally, the person he was with wheeled him away, and I sighed in relief. Then, I heard a still, small voice inside saying, *"He will be back."* If I was uneasy before, I was now sinking into a feeling of foreboding.

Near the end of the afternoon, it was my turn to preach and conclude the outreach. I dutifully preached with passion, filled with boldness and zeal. In the middle of my sermon, guess who was wheeled back in front of me? You guessed it! Now I had to contend with the noises and distractions. I felt fine about doing that, until he suddenly leaped from his wheelchair growling and scampered on all fours... right toward me. This was not good!

I cannot explain how I did what I did, but as he approached the steps, something beyond me rose up inside. I walked down the steps and met his charge with an outstretched hand. I gently laid it on his head. He stopped in his tracks and I simply said, *"In the name of Jesus, be still."* To my amazement, he quieted down and on all fours, he crawled back to his wheelchair. I wish I could tell you it was a courageous act on my part, but it was simply God honoring His promise to me from Verse 15 of Psalm 91, which says, *"I will be with him in trouble; I will deliver him and honor him."* I cannot even say I was abiding in the expectation of the supernatural intervention of God, but I think it was just God honoring the promises in His Word. I am sure that without His supernatural intervention, it would have been a different story. That memory now helps me abide in the expectation that He will do it again.

That makes an interesting testimony, but it is not the end. As I continued my sermon, amazed that I was still in one piece, I noticed the guys in front of the pool hall leering at me. I thought to myself, *"Now I am a dead man. I might as well finish with a flourish."* I ended with an altar call for salvation. Suddenly, the biggest, meanest looking of the guys standing in front of the pool hall began to walk toward me. He was a Tongan, and easily weighed three hundred and fifty pounds. I was sunk. I was sure he was going to kill me! What could I do? I just continued with my invitation to come to Christ. When this giant of a man got about six feet from me, he suddenly stopped. Then, he began to weep. For the second time that afternoon, I was taken back in amazement. I led him in a prayer for his salvation and that was that! He and I hugged and he returned to his friends.

God used those two uncomfortable, and yes, even threatening situations in an unfamiliar, far away place, to show me His power and glory. I am confident that I can anticipate the supernatural intervention of God when the situation is far bigger than I am. That day, God also showed me His heart for a lost and dying world. The experience changed me forever. I learned something about how faith will float your boat if you will allow God to navigate your course for you.

---

### LIFELINE
He will still the storms inherent in your weaknesses and shortcomings. He will perform His Word over you.

---

## Fourth Expectation: The Significance of Your Life

The fourth expectation comes from the third verse of Genesis 12. God promised Abram that he would have a truly significant life, and would affect all the families of the earth. Abram left for his journey filled with this fourth expectation. It would be the motivating promise that kept his faith strong through all his trials.

*(Genesis 12:3b NKJV) "And in you all the families of the earth shall be blessed."*

When I pray, it is not usually for success. It is that whatever I am doing would be eternally significant. (That is the true measure of success.) My desire is to have faith to stay the course. Then, when I finally sail my boat home to the other side, I will have taken with me a great cargo of fruitfulness. Let me encourage you not to settle for less. Let your fourth expectation be that your life will have a significant impact on as many as possible, so they too, would enjoy the blessings of God. You could settle for the ordinary. You could even settle for some extraordinary successes. Why not press toward something higher? Abide in the expectation of eternal, fruitful significance for your life.

This chapter started with the idea that a moral man's boat floats on having faith to seek God's direction and his determination to stay on the course God sets for him. Challenge yourself. Will you set your sail with expectations for increase, excellence, the supernatural intervention of God, and finally, the expectation that your life will have lasting significance?

# Chapter 11

# The Faith-Filled Feet of a Moral Man

As we have seen, faith is a necessary component of every moral man's journey. What faith principle will help you consistently navigate the waters of life in ways that are pleasing to God and beneficial to you? James' epistle established a truth that answers this question. Let us look at what he wrote and extract a valuable principle from his writings.

*(James 2:14-18 NKJV) "What does it profit, my brethren, if someone says he has faith but does not have works? Can faith save him? {15} If a brother or sister is naked and destitute of daily food, {16} and one of you says to them, "Depart in peace, be warmed and filled," but you do not give them the things which are needed for the body, what does it profit? {17} Thus also faith by itself, if it does not have works, is dead. {18} But someone will say, "You have faith, and I have works." Show me your faith without your works, **and I will show you my faith by my works.**"*

James writes about putting faith in motion. He teaches that we need to take our faith and do something with it. I call this "putting feet to your faith." "Putting feet to your faith" simply means that you move ahead in life with an understanding that your effectiveness, success and significance hinge on your willingness to partner your faith with action (your *"works"*). Faith alone has no ability to function. It is designed to be linked in combination with *"works."* Together, your faith and works will take you to your destiny.

Faith in motion does two notable things. First, it carries a man through the doubts and difficulties that want to stop him. Second, it strengthens his resolve to resist temptation or compromise, which will try to entice him to move away from doing what he knows is right. "Putting feet to his faith" positions a man to take actions that will overcome the challenges he faces.

Have you ever heard it said that someone was "so heavenly minded that they were no earthly good?" This phrase describes someone who feels greatly drawn to God, but has chosen not to act on what he feels. His problem is that he confines his faith to feelings, which can easily fail him. He does not demonstrate his faith with actions. Faith may be manifested as legitimate feelings, but it needs to get into our feet, so we can act accordingly and do something with it. James teaches us that we need to take our faith from the realm of feelings into the sure foundation of what we know. Then, we act on it. Always be ready to exercise your "faith feet." You will be greatly strengthened and encouraged. Even more importantly, you will please God.

*(Hebrews 11:6 NIV) "And without faith it is impossible to please God... "*

*(Hebrews 13:20-21 NKJV) "Now may the God of peace who brought up our Lord Jesus from the dead, that great Shepherd of the sheep, through the blood of the everlasting covenant, {21} make you*

*complete in every good work to do His will, working in you what is well pleasing in His sight, through Jesus Christ, to whom be glory forever and ever. Amen."*

## Faith Is…

Faith can take on many attributes. It can be described in many ways and fit each need very differently. I remember three distinct faith challenges in my own life. The first came when my wife, Nancy and I moved to Fiji.

It was 1996. We had been invited to come to Fiji to start a Bible school and a church. While still in America, we discovered that the Fijian authorities had denied my work permit. Nevertheless, we knew it was God's will to go, so we purchased our tickets and arrived on visitor's visas, full of hopeful, quiet expectation. Our visas had ninety-day limits. I started teaching our first group of students in a lean-to at the side of the offices of the denomination that invited us to come (the Christian Mission Fellowship). The eighty-eighth day arrived and I was still without a work-permit. Our visas had only two days left, but as usual, I just kept believing and continued with my teaching. I was determined to keep "putting feet to my faith," regardless of the circumstances.

On the eighty-ninth day, my quiet exercise of faith was answered, and God enabled me to keep my "faith feet" moving. Word came that the official who denied my work permit had no valid reason for doing so. He simply did not like Christians. His superiors found this out and he was relieved of his duties. I immediately received my work permit and our visa extensions. Here is the point. God is never late, but it seems that He seldom chooses to be early. Rest in your faith and abide in the expectation that He will be on time.

---

### LIFELINE
God is seldom early, but abide in the expectation that He will be on time.

---

My second example was anything but quiet. It was more like a tidal wave, about to engulf me. This testimony illustrates that when a man exercises faith in the face of overwhelming trouble, God is willing and well able to respond. He will shake up your trouble and sink it into a sea of its own destruction. It will be destroyed, not you. Here is the testimony of God's reaction to my faith walk in the face of overwhelming news.

We had recently completed our three-year commitment in Fiji and returned to America. We were planting a church in New York City. Everything was moving along and then it happened. It had been a long time since I had visited a doctor. I went for a routine physical examination. When the tests came back, the doctor unceremoniously said to me, "You have cancer. You have had it for a long time. It is like a runaway freight train heading down a hill, and will probably kill you." I felt the impact of the doctor's words and it rocked my boat. You can imagine that I needed substantially more than quiet faith. Instantly, in that moment of need, God gave Nancy and me the gift of special faith.

I needed that special faith that would steady my boat. I had to believe God for a miracle. In the midst of what became a prolonged personal storm, I simply believed God, behaved accordingly, and fully expected that He would exercise His omnipotence over the outcome. I would consider nothing else. I never allowed doubt, the devil or the cancer to have an opening that could trip up my faith. At this writing, it is more than eleven years later. Yes, I received my miracle from God.

God was as ready to perform His Word over me then, as He is over you today. Here I am, alive and healthy, still giving the devil a headache and a case of heartburn every chance I get... all to the glory of my faithful God. I live with the first-hand knowledge that He is a boat-steadying, cancer-killing and promise-keeping God. He is absolute in power, infinite in wisdom and completely dependable. He is full of grace and desires to be Ruler over every aspect of your life for your good and His glory.

In the first example, I knew the call of God and I "put feet to my faith." I did my part. In the second example, I embraced the gift of faith, prayed and drew closer to God. I believed God would do His part. I did mine.

In the third example, you will see that all I did, literally, was put feet to my faith. Nancy and I walked and prayed... and walked some more and prayed some more. We just kept doing this until God responded with His sovereign grace and absolute faithfulness.

Following my miraculous healing, Nancy and I left New York City and went back to our home church in Lake Worth, Florida so I could rest and gather my strength. I was not there long when God spoke to my heart, telling me to go back and finish what I started. Nancy and I packed up and back we went to New York City. It was the middle of winter. The Lord directed us to an area of lower Manhattan, called Union Square. It was an exceedingly difficult place to plant a church. It was expensive to rent space to hold services. People rushed about and nobody wanted to stop long enough to hear what we had to say. The buildings were guarded by uniformed doormen, and it was impossible to go door-to-door inviting people to church. What were we to do? We did the only thing we could. We walked around the Union Square neighborhood and prayed. I remember how often we prayed, *"God, we cannot do this. It is beyond our abilities. We trust You. It is in Your hands. You are faithful!"*

It was the dead of winter. The weather was bitter, wet and uncomfortable. We walked and prayed for three long, cold months. We were so cold we often had to retreat to a bookstore on the north edge of the park at Union Square. It had a coffee bar, where we would warm ourselves with hot cocoa. Then, we would go back into the weather to walk and pray some more. To this day, I cannot tell you how it happened or where the people came from, but three months later, I found myself preaching our first worship service to about forty people. We even had the help of a worship team, which was loaned to us by a church from across the river in New Jersey.

Each of these three faith challenges taught me a great lesson about navigating the waters of whatever assignment God gives. It is not important to know how God is going to do it. What is important is never to give up. Your requirement will always be to press in and press on, until God moves. Never waiver or consider retreating to a "Plan B." Stay with "Plan Alpha and Omega." Determine in your heart to keep doing what God said to do, the last time He said to do it. The beautiful feet of a faith-filled man keep walking on water until God provides further instructions.

## Beautiful Feet Set Their Sail

In 1993, I invited Ian Butterworth, a Bible school educator from New Zealand, to preach in my service. His message was from Romans 10:15. He titled it, *"How beautiful are the feet of those who preach the gospel of peace, Who bring glad tidings of good things!"* He concluded with this short poem by Eva J. Orr. Her words were planted in my heart the day I heard them. Let them find their way into your heart, and energize your feet.

*One ship sails east and one sails west*
*By the self same winds that blow.*
*It's the set of the sail and not the gale*
*That determines the way they go.*

*Like the winds of the sea are the ways of*
*time as we journey along through life.*
*It's the set of the soul that determines the*
*goal and not the calm or the strife.*

Beautiful feet belong to the faith-filled moral man who refuses to allow the winds of life, whether calm or stormy, to direct his course. He determines where he is going, and from within his heart, he sets his sail. As a man with beautiful feet, you have this same opportunity. It takes faith-filled feet to climb up and release the sail. It takes faith-filled feet to climb back down and steer the course your Navigator, the Holy Spirit has shown you. It takes faith-filled feet to glorify God. It is your choice, and you will not be able to fool yourself for long. Either you will set your sail, or it will be set by someone or something else, that has no intention of glorifying God. What will your choice be? I encourage you to set your own sail. Draw your assurance from the presence of Christ in you, who Colossians 1:27 calls *"the hope of glory."*

> ## LIFELINE
> Faith-filled feet glorify God. They are beautiful feet that never stop walking in hope.

As I often say, *"When God is glorified, the devil is horrified!"* You can live a life that says, *"I am on fire and the devil is a liar."* Why don't you look into a mirror and speak that over yourself? Let it stick in your heart and change your life. Welcome that holy fire inside of you today. Let your words ignite something.

I have to confess that it has not always been easy, but I have tried to honor this prayer, *"Lord, let my feet be beautiful, faith-filled feet."* Only after my feet had put lots of miles and a few oceans under them, did I begin to understand what I was asking. God will only answer this prayer if your feet are washed in tears for the lost and less fortunate. God will always honor such tears. As your beautiful feet journey through life, you will find a desire to add to the prayer, as I have. Perhaps such prayers as this one, which I have often prayed, will touch your heart.

*"Let my footprints be places of blessing.*

*When I have passed by, let the shadow of my presence be places of good news, healing, love, mercy and encouragement.*

*God, let the voice you give me be full of glad tidings of good things.*

*Let my life say, "Look, here is Jesus. See Him in me!""*

## Feet that Carry the Light

Shine your light. It will brighten your potential to be a moral man of great impact and influence. You will swim through sharks, lionfish and even devilfish. You will make a difference. I have often combined Jesus' words in Matthew 5:14-16 with the closing words of Proverbs 4:18. Together, these Scriptures speak of a man's purpose, hope and vision. They are great encouragers for every moral man of God.

*(Matthew 5:14-16 NKJV) "You are the light of the world. A city that is set on a hill cannot be hidden. {15} Nor do they light a lamp and put it under a basket, but on a lampstand, and it gives light to all who are*

*in the house. {16} Let your light so shine before men, that they may see your good works and glorify your Father in heaven."*

*(Proverbs 4:18 NKJV) "...the path of the just is like the shining sun, That shines ever brighter unto the perfect day."*

What kind of feet do you have today? How would you feel about asking God for beautiful feet, with even more meaningful footsteps? Go ahead and try it. You will like it. No, that is not accurate. You will love it... and be forever grateful for your beautiful, faith-filled, God-honoring, God-pleasing, God-glorifying feet! Such feet get to carry the light. Moral men have beautiful feet because their feet move the light into darkness and the darkness has to flee! Please understand the process. Jesus did not say, *"Make your light so shine..."* He said, *"Let your light so shine..."* It is not what you do; it is who you are that makes the difference. As a moral man, you are a vessel of light, a container. You are not the light. You contain the Light, the Lord Jesus Christ. The impact of your beautiful feet brilliantly will radiate your faith in Him and His Word. As you do this, the glory of the Lord will shine brightly.

In 1996, I established the School of Urban Missions in Fiji. One of my pioneering students was John Ryland. His story illustrates how the faithful, beautiful feet of a committed moral man will make a difference.

John had a heavy workload from the school, a pregnant wife and responsibilities to do outreach ministry each day after class. He was extremely busy. Nevertheless, John found time to join a local rugby team. I was concerned about how busy he had become. I asked him if he thought he had stretched himself too far. His reply was that he joined the rugby team because he knew that none of the men on the team was serving God. It was his intention to let his light shine and perhaps lead some of them to a place of commitment to the Lord. To John, this was worth whatever extra effort and time it took.

> LIFELINE
> When you consider what the Lord has done, everything you are is the least you can give.

John Ryland was a shining, living epistle on that rugby team. He faithfully worked to write himself on the hearts of those men. John also wrote himself on my heart. I watched him combine faith with his works to reveal the light within. I really do not remember if any of the team members were saved, but I do know I saw the faith of a moral man in action. John's life glorified God and absolutely and completely horrified the devil!

Writing about John Ryland has reminded me of my early days as a United States Marine. I had the privilege of serving my country in the troubling years of the Vietnam War back in the 1960's. I was well trained. I had an understanding of the weapons I would be given for the fight. When I think of John Ryland, one weapon in particular stands out from those days in Vietnam. It was called a "shaped charge." It got its name from the way it was constructed. Its builders fashioned it in such a way that it was shaped for maximum penetration of armored targets. It was harmless until it moved toward its target. When it hit, the impact was highly focused and effective. John Ryland was a Holy Ghost "shaped charge," fashioned on the Potter's wheel. He was appropriate for his target, the men of the rugby team. John's intention was to let the light of the Gospel explode among them and obliterate the works of the devil. As he ran around the rugby field with his beautiful feet, I am sure he destroyed the bondage and lies that kept some of his teammates in darkened, troubled waters. Two truths from Scripture come to mind. The first is from Roman 10:15, and the second is from 2 Corinthians 10:4. I have paraphrased both.

*How well timed, appropriate and favorable for release from destructive bondage are the explosive footsteps of moral men (such as you) who go to announce the message of peace with God.*

*For the weapons of a moral man's warfare (your faith and works combined) are not weak and carnal, but mighty in God for utterly destroying evil, as they pull down all that glorifies the devil and his vile purposes.*

## Expectant Feet

As you consider what I have written in this chapter, I invite you to go beyond the information you have read. You have more than enough information. Your mind is probably filled with a great supply of explanations concerning the Scriptures, with which you can reason for the Gospel. However, we are called to "put feet to our faith" and let our lights shine. For this to happen, we must go beyond information and explanations. Moral manhood is the condition in which a Christian man functions as a living demonstration. Information without demonstration is the stuff from which dead religion is made. Demonstration is the stuff of miracles! I love what Paul wrote to the Corinthian church from his personal shark cage of humility.

*(1 Corinthians 2:1-4 NKJV) "...my speech and my preaching were not with persuasive words of human wisdom, but in demonstration of the Spirit and of power."*

God wants your life to be a demonstration of His power and glory. Here is the correct order. First, give your demonstration, and then, you can provide the necessary information and explanation. Information and explanation certainly have their place, but the life of God and His anointing are in the demonstration. What the world needs are demonstrations, followed by information and explanations. Be a complete moral man. Be God's demonstration. Explode God's light all over someone's darkness. As you do, they will be eager to hear your explanation.

As you can see, I have given a lot of thought to what faith is. I believe my conclusions will help you understand the importance of faith in your walk on the waters of God's personal plan for your life. Here is a sampling of my conclusions of what faith is, in its infinitely varied forms. Let's begin with Hebrews 11:1.

*(Hebrews 11:1 NLT) "What is faith? It is the confident assurance that what we hope for is going to happen. It is the evidence of things we cannot yet see."*

1. My paraphrase of the New Living Translation of Hebrews 11:1 is this.

*Faith is the fully confident, unshakeable expectation, based completely on the faithfulness of God and His Word, that a moral man's hopes will arrive with God's appropriate timing. They will bring with them what he can only see in the spirit today, but will become reality in due season.*

2. I have previously given you my wife Nancy's definition of faith, which I believe is among the best I have heard. Here it is again.

*"Faith is looking into the light and holding onto what you see in the spirit, until it comes to pass."*

3. I love to remind myself of Dr. Charles Stanley's wonderful definition of faith.

*"Faith is believing God, behaving accordingly, and trusting Him for the outcomes."*

4. This one is mine.

*Faith is walking on the waters of your circumstances, with your eyes fixed solely on Jesus. You refuse to look down. You refuse to look sideways. You have made the determination only to look up. Your feet are beautiful, faith-filled and highly buoyant. You have determined not to sink. You will walk on as much water as necessary, because you are a faith-filled, moral man of God.*

# Chapter 12

## Fish for Dinner or Dinner for the Fish?

*(John 21:4-10 NKJV) "But when the morning had now come, Jesus stood on the shore; yet the disciples did not know that it was Jesus. {5} Then Jesus said to them, "Children, have you any food?" They answered Him, "No." {6} And He said to them, "Cast the net on the right side of the boat, and you will find some." So they cast, and now they were not able to draw it in because of the multitude of fish. {7} Therefore that disciple whom Jesus loved said to Peter, "It is the Lord!" Now when*

*Simon Peter heard that it was the Lord, he put on his outer garment (for he had removed it), and plunged into the sea. {8} But the other disciples came in the little boat (for they were not far from land, but about two hundred cubits), dragging the net with fish. {9} Then, as soon as they had come to land, they saw a fire of coals there, and fish laid on it, and bread. {10} Jesus said to them, "Bring some of the fish which you have just caught.""*

## What does the Lord require of you?

When our resurrected Lord appeared to the disciples on the shore of the sea, He gave them two commands. First, He required them to cast their net on the right side of the boat. They did so. When John realized who it was speaking from the shore, he said, *"It is the Lord."* I can only imagine the excitement and wonder in his voice. Peter's response was immediate. Yes, he had previously let Jesus and himself down. His failure was like a haunting memory. He had lost hope. Now, his hope resurfaced. He could not contain himself. He jumped into the sea and swam to shore. If he had thought about it, he probably could have walked on the water all the way to Jesus!

The other disciples brought the boat to shore, dragging their miracle net full of fish with them. There was Christ, welcoming them to the warmth of the fire. Now, the Lord required a second thing of them. He commanded them, *"Bring some of the fish which you have just caught."* Can you imagine the emotions they felt, as they obeyed His second command? Their obedience turned into their blessing. They had a meal of fish and bread, all supplied by the Lord. More importantly, they shared it with Him.

Jesus' two commands were connected. First, He required them to go fishing according to His instructions. Then they were to bring what they caught to Jesus. Some things never change. If you want to catch your miracle and find your way to your destiny, do what the disciples did. Simply obey God. That is what He requires of you.

What we must remember is that, even more than being successful at catching fish, Jesus trained them to be fishers of men. This is the primary requirement of God for every man who calls Jesus his Lord.

> *(Matthew 4:19 NKJV) "Then He said to them, "Follow Me, and I will make you fishers of men.""*

185

> **LIFELINE**
> If you want to catch your miracle,
> do it His way.

## Requirement Checklist

Have you considered what else the Lord might require of you, beyond being a fisher of men? The Scriptures are filled with commands for every God-fearing moral man. They form a checklist for swimming through what are the increasingly dangerous waters of life. Here are a number of commands with which you can start.

## Begin by doing Three Good Things.

The Prophet Micah's writings reveal three commands against which you can check yourself. They will help you to be certain you are meeting God's timeless requirements for a successful swim in the waters of life.

*(Micah 6:8 NKJV) "He has shown you, O man, what is good; And what does the LORD require of you But to do justly, To love mercy, And to walk humbly with your God?"*

1. *"To do justly"* simply means always to do what you know in your heart is right. You really cannot fool yourself. When you have a heart to follow God, you will know what is right. When you listen to the voice of the Holy Spirit, He will convict you not to do what is wrong. He will guide you in doing what is right.

2. *"To love mercy"* will take you beyond simply doing acts of mercy. God requires that you *"love"* mercy. This means to genuinely love being merciful to those who are less fortunate than you. He clearly commands you to *"love your neighbor as yourself."* We will look at this shortly.

3. *"To walk humbly with your God"* has two facets. First, God's fervent desire is that you *"walk"* with Him. He knows that if you will include Him as your close walking Partner in your journey through life, He will be there to speak with you and care for you. Here is the second facet. He commands every moral man to check himself and his actions against the measuring rod of humility. We discussed this in-depth in earlier chapters. Humility will keep those pride sharks away. What a combination, walking with God and embracing your humility! It is a formula for success and significance for every champion for Jesus.

Look carefully at my paraphrase of Micah 6:8.

*He has shown you, O God's champion, what is good in His eyes for you to do. What is it the LORD requires of you? (These are not suggestions. They are requirements.) First, do what you know in your heart is right. Second, become a man who genuinely loves being merciful to the less fortunate. Finally, God's desire is that you stay as close to Him as you can. Allow your life to show the same humility He did when He went to the cross for you.*

## Ten More Good Things

Moses received the Ten Commandments from God. They are timelessly foundational to the character of every moral man. They are unique among God's commandments, in that they were written by the finger of God directly into stone. That certainly got Moses' attention. The same God who wrote them to Moses deserves our attention as well. He is who He says He is. He never changes, nor does His Word. He is worthy of complete reverence, respect and honor.

*(Deuteronomy 10:1-4 NKJV) ""At that time the LORD said to me, 'Hew for yourself two tablets of stone like the first, and come up to*

*Me on the mountain and make yourself an ark of wood. {2} And I will write on the tablets the words that were on the first tablets, which you broke; and you shall put them in the ark.' {3} So I made an ark of acacia wood, hewed two tablets of stone like the first, and went up the mountain, having the two tablets in my hand. {4} And He wrote on the tablets according to the first writing, the Ten Commandments, which the LORD had spoken to you in the mountain from the midst of the fire in the day of the assembly; and the LORD gave them to me."*

## The Ten Commandments
### (Exodus 20:3-17)

| Verse | | Commandment |
|---|---|---|
| 20:3 | *1* | *"You shall have no other gods before Me."* |
| 20:4 | *2* | *"You shall not make for yourself a carved image, or any likeness of anything that is in heaven above, or that is in the earth beneath, or that is in the water under the earth;"* |
| 20:7 | *3* | *"You shall not take the name of the LORD your God in vain"* |

| 20:8 | 4 | *"Remember the Sabbath day, to keep it holy. {9} Six days you shall labor and do all your work, {10} but the seventh day is the Sabbath. In it you shall do no work."* |
| | | (In the New Covenant, Jesus used His authority to bring grace to the Sabbath. It could now be observed as a time of rest and fellowship with God, not a religious work.) |
| | | *(Luke 6:5 NKJV) "And He said to them, "The Son of Man is also Lord of the Sabbath.""* |
| 20:12 | 5 | *"Honor your father and your mother, that your days may be long upon the land which the LORD your God is giving you."* |
| 20:13 | 6 | *"You shall not murder."* |
| 20:14 | 7 | *"You shall not commit adultery."* |
| 20:15 | 8 | *"You shall not steal."* |
| 20: 16 | 9 | *"You shall not bear false witness against your neighbor."* |
| 20:17 | 10 | *"You shall not covet…"* |

Every man who truly serves Christ is to honor these Ten Commandments and the three from

Micah 6:8. Remember, these are not "The Ten Suggestions" and "Three Requests!"

## His Greatest Commandment: The Royal Law of Love

*(Matthew 22:36-40 NKJV) "Teacher, which is the great commandment in the law?" {37} Jesus said to him, "'You shall love the LORD your God with all your heart, with all your soul, and with all your mind.' {38} This is the first and great commandment. {39} And the second is like it: 'You shall love your neighbor as yourself.' {40} On these two commandments hang all the Law and the Prophets."*

The Lord Jesus Christ gave the Royal Law of Love first priority among all His commandments. Therefore, love Him first, and then second, love your neighbor. Let your approach to all the other biblical commandments be guided and measured by these two. Stay on course. Set your priorities correctly and you will successfully set your sail to take you to your destiny. Look honestly at yourself. Do your attitudes and actions give evidence of your uncompromising submission to God's Royal Law of Love?

> ### LIFELINE
> God's kind of love is a life-preserver.

I am sure you have experienced the reality that love is not always convenient. However, it is always a command. I admit that it is a command I sometimes find challenging to obey. I have always been task oriented. At times, this can be a good thing. However, being task oriented can sometimes distract you from what really counts, those people God has given you to love and care for. They are always more important than the task at hand. I used to struggle with this more than I do today. Admittedly, there are times when I am still tempted to neglect the people around me for my interest in some task. There was a time when God graciously provided me with a teachable moment in which I realized my priorities were wrong. Let me explain.

It was during my time pastoring in the Fiji Islands. I had an office in my home in which I spent hours preparing sermons and Bible school lessons. I have always enjoyed my times of study and preparation. I would become intensely involved in what I was doing. I had little tolerance for being interrupted.

I was hard at work one afternoon getting ready for Sunday's message. The revelation was flowing and I was into some seriously satisfying study and writing. Suddenly there was a knock at the front door of our home. I can remember grumbling to myself, *"What is going to interrupt me now?"* My wife Nancy appeared at my office door and said something like this, *"Some of our students have come to visit. They brought food and want to spend time with us."* I was immediately irritated and resented the interruption, but knew I had to go out and greet them. Perhaps I could quickly excuse myself and get back to work.

When I walked into our parlor, there they were, smiling from ear to ear. *"Pastor Bob, we just want to bless you and sister Nancy. We brought food and are here to visit with you."* In that moment, my heart melted, as God impressed me with the reality that He had given me these wonderful people to love and care for. The students were the gift from God that forever changed me. They were the most important thing in the world to Him, and I realized they would now be the same to me. I forgot about sermon preparation and jumped into the fellowship with both feet. It was a joyful, glorious time.

That afternoon forever changed me. The exercise of God's Royal Law of Love became more than a commandment for me. It was a God-given opportunity. I realized that neglect of His Royal Law is immoral, ill advised, and to put it bluntly, just plain stupid. Yes, it bears repeating. Failure to love as God does is just plain stupid. The only thing I will take with me into eternity is how my life touched others. It is still not always easy to give people priority over things I want to do. I sometimes fail, but most of the time, I succeed. The greatest benefit to me is what it has done in my heart. I am not the same as I was when working at my desk in Fiji those many years ago. I no longer regard doing things (no matter how important they seem) above spending time with God's incredible people. I understand the value of God's kind of love at work in my heart. I hope reading this gives you pause to consider how much priority the exercise of His love has in your heart.

*(1 Corinthians 13:8 NKJV) "Love never fails. But whether there are prophecies, they will fail; whether there are tongues, they will cease; whether there is knowledge, it will vanish away."*

194

# What about You?

Now that you have read this, stop and take the time to ask, *"Lord, what do you want me to do?"* I have tried to establish this question as a priority as I prepare for my day. The question is not original to me. Many of God's servants throughout the Bible asked it, but I have been particularly inspired by one of them.

> *(Acts 9:3-6 NKJV) "As he journeyed he came near Damascus, and suddenly a light shone around him from heaven. {4} Then he fell to the ground, and heard a voice saying to him, "Saul, Saul, why are you persecuting Me?" {5} And he said, "Who are You, Lord?" Then the Lord said, "I am Jesus, whom you are persecuting. It is hard for you to kick against the goads." {6} So he, trembling and astonished, said, **"Lord, what do You want me to do?"** Then the Lord said to him, "Arise and go into the city, and you will be told what you must do.""*

---

**LIFELINE**
If you ask, He will tell you what to do.

---

You see, it is all about perspective and attitude. If you want to avoid the inside of the frying pan, you can do so by being the moral man God designed you to be. You will enjoy the fellowship of many fish dinners, because you obeyed all that God required of you. You will never be dinner for the fish.

# Chapter 13

## The Fear of the Lord

*(Ecclesiastes 12:13-14 NKJV) "Let us hear the conclusion of the whole matter: Fear God and keep His commandments, For this is man's all. {14} For God will bring every work into judgment, Including every secret thing, Whether good or evil."*

Throughout the book, I have invited you to look at many issues that make or break a moral man's life. In some way, I have shown they all relate to the kinds of choices you make concerning your character. You have seen it is impossible to separate character choices from faith choices. To these, I now want to add a third choice, which is your decision to *"Fear God and keep His commandments."* Stay with me as we add the fear of the Lord to the requirements for godly character and faith. This completes what is necessary for a moral man's swim through the waters of life.

Let's dive deeply into what I have found to be the ultimate game-changer, the fear of the Lord. It has the power, when added to your unwavering character and faith choices, to be the full guarantee that will take you safely to the end of your journey.

Often, the fear of the Lord is not clearly or properly defined. It is taught in a watered-down way. Some men try to justify or excuse themselves by defining it to fit their own lifestyle choices. Consider the difference between our two friends from Chapter 7, Fred Finfool and Daniel. How did the fear of the Lord determine their differences? Fred Finfool displayed no fear of the Lord. He lived a defiled lifestyle. Daniel feared God. He was a moral man who consistently honored the Lord.

## What is the fear of the Lord?

My pastor, Dr. Tom Peters, has an excellent, comprehensive definition of the fear of the Lord.

> *"The fear of the Lord is to esteem, honor, and hold Him in highest regard; as well as to venerate, stand in awe and reverence Him. It is to tremble with the greatest respect for Him, His presence and His commands, as well as His wishes."*[5]

---

[5] Dr. Peters' sermon of September 19, 2010 at Trinity Church International, Lake Worth, Florida, USA.

Let's break Dr. Peters' definition into two parts. The first is commonly held and certainly accurate. As Dr. Peters says, we *are "to esteem, honor, and hold the Lord in highest regard; as well as to venerate, stand in awe and reverence Him."* This part of the definition comes from an understanding of the loving, righteous character of God, in all the beauty of His holiness. When a man accepts this definition as a part-time, optional principle for life, it leaves room for him to ignore the full range of God's attributes. It only provides a partial picture. It opens the door to the self-justification of his sinful behavior because it diminishes the true, complete picture of God. Look at the second half of Dr. Peters' definition. It must be regarded as inseparable from the first half.

*"It is **to tremble with the greatest respect** for Him, His presence and His commands, as well as His wishes."*

Here are three key points to this second half of the definition. They are vital to you because they will drive you deeply into your proper place of worship and respect for God. As God's champion, you will profit highly from this correct sense of the fear of the Lord. You will position yourself for a victorious life. Here are the three points.

1. Your understanding of God's person will be so accurate and strong that it drives you to

*"tremble with the greatest respect"* before Him. You leave no room for intentional sin. It will find no place in your heart.

2.  Your understanding of God's place in your life will drive you to honor His presence as an incredible gift. You will give no opening for insolence or deliberate arrogance to abide within your heart. You will gratefully fall at His feet and cry "holy." It will be settled in your heart that the set of your sail is purely to catch the wind of His Spirit.

3.  Fear of the Lord will be the catalyst for your obedience. It will guide you into appropriate responses to His commands, desires and wishes. You will know that your obedience and submission invite His perfect will. You will be a man who determines not to have any choice but faithful obedience. If He says it, that's it, because He has absolute dominion. He is God. You are not! You will gladly wear the honor of being His bondservant.

There are a number of places in Scripture that the fear of the Lord is mentioned. The use of this term by the Holy Spirit, through Scripture's anointed writers, gives understanding of the depths of its meanings. You can make a checklist for your own life from these meanings.

# Checklist for Life

☑ The fear of the Lord is uncontaminated by worldly lusts or thinking. Nothing has polluted it. It is holy.

> *(Psalms 19:9 NIV) "The fear of the LORD is pure,"*

☑ The fear of the Lord is the starting point to acquire wisdom for life. It is tied directly to obedience to God's Word.

> *(Psalms 111:10 NKJV) "The fear of the LORD is the beginning of wisdom; A good understanding have all those who do His commandments. His praise endures forever."*

> *(Proverbs 1:7 NKJV) "The fear of the LORD is the beginning of knowledge, But fools despise wisdom and instruction."*

☑ The proper and complete fear of the Lord sets you in humble agreement with God. You hate what the Lord hates. You love what the Lord loves. You are like Christ in every way you can be. Your words are blessings, bringing life to those who hear them.

*(Proverbs 8:13 NKJV) "The fear of the LORD is to hate evil; Pride and arrogance and the evil way And the perverse mouth I hate."*

☑ The fear of the Lord is your divine insurance policy against prematurely being snared by death. It is a fountain that continually provides a flow of abundant life-giving resources.

*(Proverbs 14:27 NKJV) "The fear of the LORD is a fountain of life, to turn one away from the snares of death."*

☑ The fear of the Lord is a treasure from the Lord. It gives you revelation of what is holy and right in God's eyes. It opens the doors to wisdom and knowledge, which is the strength of your salvation.

*(Proverbs 9:10 NKJV) "The fear of the LORD is the beginning of wisdom, And the knowledge of the Holy One is understanding."*

*(Isaiah 33:6 NKJV) "Wisdom and knowledge will be the stability of your times, And the strength of salvation; The fear of the LORD is His treasure."*

# The Ways of Wisdom

King
Solomon

The checklist above shows there is an unbreakable connection between the fear of the Lord, and wisdom for you. If you are to navigate the waters of life successfully, you must rely on the wisdom God gives you. The world's wisdom will inevitably fail you. God's wisdom carries the guarantees you have just read. The wisest man the world has known, King Solomon, wrote this to his son about the value of wisdom, and the need to seek for it.

*(Proverbs 4:5-9 NKJV) "Get wisdom! Get understanding! Do not forget, nor turn away from the words of my mouth. {6} Do not forsake her, and she will preserve you; Love her, and she will keep you. {7} **Wisdom is the principal thing;** Therefore get wisdom. And in all your getting, get understanding. {8} Exalt her, and she will promote you; She*

*will bring you honor, when you embrace her. {9} She will place on your head an ornament of grace; A crown of glory she will deliver to you."*

Take a firm hold on wise biblical instruction. Never release or so much as ease your grasp on it. Depend on it. Allow it to be your life-long companion. Make it *"the principle thing."* Welcome and embrace its ability to bring godly increase to your life. It will govern how you feel about yourself and how your presence affects others around you.

Near the end of his days, King Solomon realized how wasteful and futile his life had been. In the Book of Ecclesiastes, he wrote to his son about the futility of a man's vanity. He knew he had blown his opportunities and understood most of his life was wasted trying to satisfy himself. Look again at Ecclesiastes 12:13-14, in which King Solomon, combining the wisdom of God and the experience of his own foolish mistakes, arrived at this conclusion.

*(Ecclesiastes 12:13-14 NKJV) "Let us hear the conclusion of the whole matter: Fear God and keep His commandments, For this is man's all. {14} For God will*

*bring every work into judgment, Including every secret thing, Whether good or evil."*

The fear of the Lord will be your best defense against the temptations and fears that confront every moral man. The sum of all biblical wisdom for life is no more and no less than that your journey be filled with opportunities to *"Fear God and keep His commandments."*

---

### LIFELINE
*"Fear God and keep His commandments."*

---

# Chapter 14

## LIFELINES

---

lifeline[6] .../luyf'luyn'/*n.*
1.  a line or rope for saving life, as one attached to a lifeboat.
2.  any of various lines running above the decks, spars, etc., of a ship or boat to give sailors something to grasp when there is danger of falling or being washed away.
3.  the line by which a diver is lowered and raised.
4.  any of several anchored lines used by swimmers for support.

---

As you navigated your way through this book, you encountered numerous LIFELINES. My purpose for each of the LIFELINES has been to provide a set of principles you can apply to your personal journey through life. As you can see from the dictionary definition, LIFELINES can serve you in a number of ways. They can link you with a way to safety in times of danger. They can also provide you with something dependable to grasp when things around

---

[6] The Eurofield Word Solutions WordGenius Dictionary, Incorporating Random House Webster's College Dictionary Content, EIS eComPress.

you get rough. Finally, they can help you get through the ups and downs you surely will encounter in the life required of a moral man who serves God.

As the book draws to a close, here is a summary of the LIFELINES you have seen. Please take the time to meditate on them individually and ask the Lord to speak to your heart concerning their collective message and potential value to you.

The character of manhood is defined by undemanding love.

(Page 3)

Your attitude about others in your care directly affects your successes in life.

(Page 44)

Your attitude about those who are vulnerable to you directly affects their lives and well-being.

(Page 45)

Sow seeds motivated by your love. You will reap a full harvest motivated by God's love.

(Page 46)

Be a reflection of Jesus. Humble yourself
and give of yourself without regard to
personal cost.

(Page 47)

Do not settle for less than 100% of the
character of God in your life. Make every
course adjustment He commands.

(Page 51)

Your holiness is personal, but its test of
authenticity is completely interpersonal.

(Page 59)

Personal holiness requires that you resist any
attraction to, or tolerance for, the unholy.

(Page 60)

Personal holiness grows, as you embrace a hunger
for change - daily, hourly and minute-by-minute.

(Page 61)

God's perfect love drives out and utterly
obliterates fear.

(Page 70)

Release God's grace from within you and it will
drive away the sharks from around you.

(Page 72)

God is completely dependable, and fully able to
consume what tries to consume you.

(Page 75)

Surrender to change. It will be liberating,
empowering and will release your destiny to you.

(Page 89)

Trust your journey to the excellence of your faith.
Trust the outcomes to the excellence of God.

(Page 94)

A moral man of excellent spirit bends to the
will of God alone.

(Page 104)

Men of excellence do not dress for the furnace.
They dress for success.

(Page 109)

Walk with Jesus. You will stand the heat.

(Page 111)

A moral man's only issue is not what he is going through. His only issue is to be faithful to the One who is going through it with him.

(Page 115)

There are no surprises in heaven, but there are multitudes of wonderful surprises from heaven.

(Page 116)

Look for God's new thing. It is yours.

(Page 138)

Maintain your confession and He will watch over your course.

(Page 146)

To succeed, you must disturb the present.

(Page 150)

Growth is fully a function of the future.

(Page 151)

He will still the storms inherent in your weaknesses and shortcomings. He will perform His Word over you.

(Page 160)

God is seldom early, but abide in the
expectation that He will be on time.

(Page 167)

Faith-filled feet glorify God. They are
beautiful feet that never stop walking in hope.

(Page 173)

When you consider what the Lord has done,
everything you are is the least you can give.

(Page 176)

If you want to catch your miracle, do it His way.

(Page 186)

God's kind of love is a life-preserver.

(Page 192)

If you ask, He will tell you what to do.

(Page 195)

*"Fear God and keep His commandments"*

(Page 205)

# Dr. Bob Abramson

Dr. Abramson has extensive experience in cross-cultural men's issues. He and his wife Nancy have pastored multicultural, international churches in New York City and the Fiji Islands in the South Pacific. He established or taught in Bible schools and ministry training centers in New Zealand, Fiji, Taiwan, Hong Kong, Malaysia, Europe and the United States. His website, "Mentoring Ministry" provides free resources worldwide.

Dr. Abramson earned a Doctor of Ministry from Erskine Theological Seminary, a Masters in Religion from Liberty University and a Bachelor of Arts in the Bible with a minor in Systematic Theology from Southeastern University. He and his wife Nancy live in Lake Worth, Florida. They have five grown children and six grandchildren.

If you wish to contact Dr. Abramson, please visit www.mentoringministry.com or write him at Dr.Bob@mentoringministry.com

Dr. Abramson is also the author of these books.
- "Just a Little Bit More - The Heart of a Mentor" (Book and Workbook)
- "The Leadership Puzzle" (Two Workbooks and Facilitator's Manual)
- "Growing Together, Marriage Enrichment for Every Culture." (Book and Workbook)

Coming soon: Reflections, Volumes 1 and 2, the first in a series of devotional journals

www.ingramcontent.com/pod-product-compliance
Lightning Source LLC
LaVergne TN
LVHW011224080426
835509LV00005B/298